Napoleon Hill was born in Virginia, USA, and died in 1970 after a long and successful career as a consultant to business leaders, lecturer and author. Hill's all-time bestseller *Think and Grow Rich*, first published in 1937, made him a millionaire in his own right and, having sold 15 million copies worldwide, set the standard for today's motivational thinking. Hill also established the Napoleon Hill Foundation, a non-profit educational institution whose mission is to promote his philosophy of leadership, self-motivation and individual achievement.

Patricia G. Horan is a 30-year veteran of New York book and magazine publishing, as well as an award-winning author, editor, copywriter and playwright. She most recently worked as an editor of *Breakthrough*, the quarterly journal of Global Education Associates, a UN non-governmental organisation founded in 1973. She is the author of *177 Favorite Poems for Children* and *Haiti: Vibrant Land of Joy and Sorrow*.

Also by Napoleon Hill from Vermilion

Think and Grow Rich
Master Key to Riches

SUCCESS

The Best of Napoleon Hill

NAPOLEON HILL

Revised and updated by

Patricia G. Horan

Vermilion
LONDON

1 3 5 7 9 10 8 6 4 2

Text taken from *The Magic Ladder to Success*, originally published 1930, and
The Law of Success, originally published 1928, by The Ralston University Press

This edition first published in 2008 by Vermilion,
an imprint of Ebury Publishing

Ebury Publishing is a Random House Group company

The Random House Group Limited Reg. No. 954009

Addresses for companies within the Random House Group can be found at
www.rbooks.co.uk

A CIP catalogue record for this book is available from the British Library

The Random House Group Limited supports The Forest Stewardship
Council (FSC), the leading international forest certification organisation.
All our titles that are printed on Greenpeace approved FSC certified paper
carry the FSC logo. Our paper procurement policy can be found at
www.rbooks.co.uk/environment

Typeset by SX Composing DTP, Rayleigh, Essex
Printed and bound in Great Britain by
CPI Cox & Wyman, Reading, RG1 8EX

ISBN 978 0 09 191708 1

Copies are available at special rates for bulk orders.
Contact the sales development team on 020 7840 8487 or visit
www.booksforpromotions.co.uk for more information.

To buy books by your favourite authors and register for offers, visit
www.rbooks.co.uk

CONTENTS

FOREWORD

In this book are the success secrets of magnates, tycoons, moguls and captains of industry. They are towering figures whose names live in history, not in infamy. Unlike the headline-makers of today, they are geniuses, not jailbirds; winners, not whiners. They had more than clout – they had class. Though they were by no means saints, they were undoubtedly larger than life; often doing what others said couldn't be done. We need their wisdom more than ever. They were the stuff of legends.

How did they – Andrew Carnegie, Alexander Graham Bell, Henry Ford, P.T. Barnum – do it? Many of them were born into impoverished circumstances. What personal alchemy turned their less-than-promising beginnings into pure gold? What is it that makes a winner?

Out of the same unforgiving circumstances came a man who set out to find the answers to this central question. With a letter of introduction from Carnegie himself, he found out these secrets by doing what no one had thought to do before: he asked the greatest how they became great. In the process, against all odds, he became a winner himself. He invented motivational writing, ultimately finding himself listed as a peer with

Marcus Aurelius, Ralph Waldo Emerson and Ben Franklin.

He was five-foot-six and his name was Napoleon, but no Waterloo ever defeated him and he refused to languish in exile. Napoleon Hill was the guru of all success gurus, and the author of the number one motivational seller of all time, *Think and Grow Rich*, which would never have seen the light of day without the original version of the book you are holding in your hands. (*Think and Grow Rich* might not have seen the light of success, either, if the publisher's choice of title had prevailed, since it would have been known as *Use Your Noodle to Earn More Boodle!*)

More than 40 years after it was published, a *USA Today* survey of business leaders named *Think and Grow Rich* one of the most inspirational business books ever and one of the five most influential books in its field. The same magical material contained in that book can be found in this one. *The Magic Ladder of Success*, which is the basis of this book, was published at the start of the Great Depression, seven years before *Think and Grow Rich,* so its chance at success was washed away along with the American economy. But the ideas in this book proved themselves to be great, and they seeded the better-known book to follow. In *Magic Ladder,* Hill's famous 17 Laws of Success were tried, tested and found to work miracles. In this new, updated version of his book – as in the original – Napoleon Hill brings together wisdom straight from the minds of the greatest names in American business history, the result of 100 interviews with the business giants of Hill's time.

In 1908, steel magnate Andrew Carnegie, son of penniless Scottish immigrants, stood in the library of his 124-room New York City mansion. He took his gold watch from his pocket and gave the young Napoleon Hill a challenge. The 25-year-old reporter had been commissioned by former Tennessee Governor Robert L. Taylor to write success stories about business leaders for his magazine. Carnegie would be his first assignment, and the steel baron had already spent three days and nights with Hill. Carnegie saw something in Hill he liked – a younger, shorter reflection of himself, perhaps – and now it was his turn to ask the questions.

Would Hill be interested in compiling the beliefs and practices of the business giants of the time into a coherent philosophy? Without any payment?

Napoleon Hill took 29 seconds to answer. 'Good,' Carnegie said as he put away his watch. 'I was planning on giving you only 60 seconds.'

Perhaps it was that incident that confirmed Hill's belief that 'Successful people make decisions quickly and change them slowly. Unsuccessful people make decisions slowly and change them often.'

Napoleon Hill would go on to become an advisor to President Franklin Delano Roosevelt. He later took credit for writing 'We have nothing to fear but fear itself' and several of FDR's famous Fireside Chats. His life would prove to be more a roller coaster than a yellow brick road: several of his businesses went bankrupt, he lost jobs, and he was wrongly accused of fraud and put into prison. One of his two sons was born without ears, and Hill's work took him away from his family so much that one of his sons was adopted by a family member.

His life was such a series of victorious failures that, when in his 50s, he marvelled that an entire decade had gone by without his having to face a personal disaster. But Napoleon Hill, often down but never out, never wavered from his Definite Chief Aim. He was to teach millions around the world that even luck can be changed and failures put to good use. How else would he have known that first-hand?

'Success requires no explanation. Failure permits no alibis,' he would later say with the authority only experience can offer.

Napoleon Hill was born in 1883 in a one-room cabin in the hills of aptly named Wise County, Virginia. A wild, gun-toting child, he began his writing career at the age of 13 as a 'mountain reporter' for small-town newspapers, and never lost his hunger for facts about real people who overcame odds. It was this childhood job that taught him how to interview the people whose philosophies of success are distilled into this book's coherent wisdom.

His is one of those it-seemed-to-be-bad-but-it-turned-out-good stories. His mother died when he was very young, but the educated, audacious woman his father then married was impatient with poverty, as he later put it. Hill's stepmother took responsibility for the family store and farm, sent his father to dental school at the age of 40 and gave Napoleon the backbone he needed to climb out of his Virginia mountain. She placed in his mind the thought he would become most famous for: 'What the mind of man can conceive, he can achieve.'

The qualities of thought that propelled the titans of yesterday are rare today, and would be most welcome in our world of instant gratification and greed. Among these are the politically incorrect concept of doing more than one is paid for, the unashamed use of 'innate spiritual powers', the idea of boldly grasping the 'big ideas' behind the principle of 'definiteness of purpose', and trusting the mind's magnetic quality. Hill encouraged 'the state of mind known as faith', and said that it frees the mind from negative traits, such as doubt and procrastination. 'The doubting mind is not a creative mind,' he says, and adds that 'Tolerance may not be your duty, but it is your privilege!' Even the highest-minded ideas are practical steps on the Magic Ladder to Success. Hill tells us, for instance, that

'Intolerance closes the doorway to opportunity in a thousand ways, and shuts out the light of intelligence.'

Hill urges us to draw freely upon the Power of Infinite Intelligence, and makes the bold observation that the greatest leaders are the most sexually driven. But he considers pure love, too, as a real source of power, sometimes referring to it in a refreshingly old-fashioned way as 'the love of sweethearts'.

Over the years, Napoleon Hill gave his name and energies to several magazines, seven books in many languages, a foundation, a film and countless lectures in many countries, franchises and tapes. The likes of Dale Carnegie, Norman Vincent Peale and Oral Roberts became devotees and sometimes shared speaking platforms with Hill. W. Clement Stone, Earl Nightingale, Denis Waitley, Zig Ziglar, Tony Robbins and others have acknowledged their enormous debt to Hill, the greatest success specialist of them all.

Insert the name Napoleon Hill into an Amazon.com book search today and nearly 18,000 references come up. Why? Because the motivational guru never fails to be quoted in books whose subjects are as wide-ranging as diet, pentathlons, communication, simple abundance, JFK, teens, online trading, feng shui, leadership, taking a band on the road, Zen and countless more. He succeeded in making his name as famous as those he interviewed.

Napoleon Hill began with nothing, learned the

secrets of those who embodied success, gained and lost a few wives and several fortunes, and died a fulfilled man in November 1970, at the age of 87.

His tombstone could very well have quoted the other famous Napoleon:

To hell with circumstances. I create circumstance.

Patricia G. Horan

AUTHOR'S ACKNOWLEDGEMENTS FROM THE ORIGINAL EDITION

This volume is the result of an analysis of the life work of over 100 men and women who have attained outstanding success in their respective callings and of over 20,000 men and women who were classed as failures.

In his labours of research and analysis the author received valuable assistance, either in person or by studying their life work, from the following men: Henry Ford, John Burroughs, Luther Burbank, Thomas A. Edison, Harvey S. Firestone, John D. Rockefeller, Charles M. Schwab, Woodrow Wilson, William Wrigley, Jr., A.D. Lasker, E.A. Filene, John Wanamaker, Marshall Field, William Howard Taft, F.W. Woolworth, George Eastman, Charles P. Stienmetz, Theodore Roosevelt and Alexander Graham Bell.

Perhaps Henry Ford and Andrew Carnegie should be acknowledged as having contributed most to the building of this philosophy. It was Mr Carnegie who first suggested writing it and Henry Ford whose life work has supplied much of the material and served, in other ways, to prove the soundness of the entire philosophy.

Napoleon Hill

AUTHOR'S ORIGINAL INTRODUCTORY STATEMENT

Napoleon Hill's Fascinating Past

I was born in the mountains of the South, surrounded by the poverty and illiteracy that were firmly established on both sides of my family. For three generations before me my ancestors were content to be poor and ignorant. I would have surely followed in their footsteps if I hadn't been blessed with an educated stepmother who came from a cultured family. Poverty and illiteracy irritated her, and she was not bashful about saying so.

My stepmother voluntarily assumed the task of planting ambition in our family, starting with my father, whom she sent away to college at the age of 40! She then proceeded to manage what passed for a 'farm' and the little country store we owned, also taking on the full support of five children: three of her own, my brother and myself. Her example made a deep and lasting impression on me.

It was she who firmly planted the seed of a life-changing idea in my young mind 30 years ago. It came in the form of a simple but unforgettable remark. With it came the idea that I could whip poverty and illiteracy, in spite of everything. That seed of an idea found a permanent home in my mind.

It was my stepmother who taught me the value of having a definite, major aim in life. Later that principle became so obviously essential a factor in the achievement of success that I gave it second place in the list of 17 principles outlined in this book, which I have been writing for a quarter of a century. This volume is the result of an analysis of the life work both of men and women who have attained outstanding success and of men and women who were classed as 'failures'.

There are several reasons why this work could not have been completed earlier. First is the scope of my self-appointed task: to learn, through decades of research, exactly what it was that others had discovered about failure and success.

Second, and equally important, is that I had to prove I could make the Law of Success philosophy work for *myself* before offering it to readers.

When I began organising the material for the Law of Success, I had no intention of creating a philosophy that you will find in this volume. In the beginning my purpose was to inform myself as to how other people had acquired wealth, so that I might follow their example.

But as the years passed I found myself becoming more eager for knowledge than for wealth, until my thirst for knowledge became so great that I practically lost sight of my original motive: financial gain.

In addition to the influence of my stepmother, I was fortunate enough to meet and gather such knowledge from the legendary Alexander Graham Bell and Andrew Carnegie, who not only further influenced me to continue my research, but supplied me with much of the important scientific data to be found in the Law of Success philosophy.

Later I met many others of high accomplishment who not only encouraged me to continue building a philosophy of success, but gave me full benefit of their own rich experiences.

I have mentioned these details for what I believe to be a very important reason: namely, the fact that the difference between success and failure is often (if not, in fact, always) determined by definite environmental influences that may be usually traced to one person.

In my case this person was my stepmother.

If it had not been for her influence in planting the seed of ambition in my mind, I never would have written a philosophy of success that is now rendering useful service to millions of people in every civilised country on earth.

While the Law of Success was still in the experimental stage, and as a part of my plan for giving it a practical trial before publishing it in textbooks, I personally passed it on, through lectures, to no fewer than 100,000 people.

Many whom I know to have received their first impulse of ambition from these lectures have since become wealthy, although some of them may have lost sight of the cause of their prosperity.

The Law of Success has been translated into countless foreign languages and taught around the world. Millions of people have been fired with ambition to whip poverty and to gain for themselves better stations in life. Moreover, this is most decidedly an age of scientific discovery, which has put sound legs under the 17 principles of the Law of Success, thus giving it a standing that it did not enjoy years ago. Today there is a very definite demand for a solid programme of success that will inspire people with higher hopes and ambitions for personal achievement.

Looking back, I have encountered great struggle and hardship, poverty and failure. But these challenges have been more than offset by the joy and prosperity I have helped others to obtain.

Not long ago, I received a letter from a former president of the United States, who congratulated me for sticking to my job for a quarter of a century, and suggested that I must feel very proud to have 'arrived' at the top of the mountain of success in time to enjoy the fruits of my labours. His letter brought to my mind the thought that one never 'arrives', if one continues to search for knowledge, because we no sooner reach the top of one peak than we discover that there are still higher mountains yet to be scaled in the distance.

No, I have not 'arrived', but I have found happiness in abundance and financial prosperity sufficient for my needs, solely through having lost myself in service to others who were earnestly struggling to find themselves. It seems worthy of mention that I did not prosper greatly until I became more concerned about spreading the Law of Success philosophy, where it would help others, than I was about accumulating money.

Don't Read this Book without Reading this First

Be sure you have a pencil and paper to hand when you begin this book. And don't attempt to read it at bedtime.

Be ready. As millions before you will testify, this book will cause important ideas to flash into your mind. As they've read these pages, inventors have been surprised and dazzled by their inventive ideas; speeches have sprung to life; business decisions have taken a bold new turn; ingenious new businesses have suddenly appeared possible.

The Law of Success philosophy is a mind magnet for brilliant ideas.

The real value of this book is not in its pages, but in your own reaction to what you read. The main purpose of the Law of Success philosophy is to stimulate the imaginative faculties of the brain so they will readily create new and usable ideas for any emergency in life.

And anyone who can create great ideas – as readers of this book tend to do – will gather great power.

As you read, underline or highlight all statements that prompt new ideas to flash into your mind. This method will serve to fix such ideas in your mind permanently. You cannot assimilate the entire subject matter of this philosophy at one reading of this book. Read it many times, and at each reading follow the habit of marking the lines that inspire new ideas.

Following this procedure will reveal to you one of the great mysteries of the human mind. Experience has proven that it will introduce you to a source of knowledge that can only be known by those who discover it themselves. You have just received a hint about the nature of the secret of the Law of Success philosophy throughout the world.

Many years of success with this book have proven that only the methods here described lead to the possession of this secret. No other.

The 17 Principles of the Law of Success

When you can acquire whatever you want without violating the rights of others, you possess power . . . the only genuine power.

This basic course presents the simple principles through which such power has been attained by those who have become successful – even astonishingly so.

These principles are not only invaluable in business, but will be financially productive in solving one's economic problems, no matter what the calling or field.

The factors through which power may be acquired and used in harmony with the above definition are 17 in number:

1. The Master Mind
2. The Importance of a Definite Aim
3. Self-confidence
4. The Habit of Saving
5. Initiative and Leadership
6. Imagination
7. Enthusiasm
8. Self-control
9. The Habit of Doing More than Paid for
10. The Personality of Success
11. Accurate Thinking
12. Concentration
13. Cooperation
14. Profiting by Failure
15. Tolerance
16. Using the Golden Rule to Win Cooperation
17. The Habit of Health

Let us begin with a complete analysis of each of these 17 proven success principles.

CHAPTER 1

THE MASTER MIND

The Master Mind principle may be defined as 'a composite mind, consisting of two or more individual minds working in perfect harmony, with a Definite Aim in view'.

Keep in mind the definition of success, the result of the application of power, and you will more quickly grasp the meaning of the term Master Mind. It will be immediately obvious that a group of two or more minds, working in harmony and perfectly coordinated, will create power in abundance.

All success is achieved through the application of power. The starting point, however, may be described as a burning desire for the achievement of some specific, definite objective.

Just as the oak tree, in the embryo, sleeps within the acorn, success begins in the form of an intense desire. Out of strong desires grow the motivating forces that cause the ambitious to cherish hopes, build plans, develop courage and stimulate their minds to a highly intensified degree of action in pursuit of some definite plan or purpose.

Desire, Don't Wish

Desire, then, is the starting point of all human achievement. At the heart of desire lie certain stimuli, through which the desire is fanned into a hot flame of action. These stimuli are known and will be listed later as a part of the Law of Success philosophy described in this book.

It has been said, and not without reason, that one may have anything one wants, within reasonable limitations, providing one wants it badly enough! Anyone who is capable of stimulating his or her mind to an intense state of desire is also capable of more than average achievement in the pursuit of that desire. It must be remembered that wishing for a thing is not the same as desiring it. A wish is merely a passive form of desire. Only out of intense desire will impelling forces of action grow, driving one to build plans and put those plans to work. Most people never advance beyond the 'wishing' stage.

The Power Motivators

One or more of the following eight basic motivating forces – the stimuli mentioned above – is the starting point of all human achievement worth noting:

1. The urge towards self-preservation
2. The desire for sexual contact
3. The desire for financial gain
4. The desire for life after death
5. The desire for fame; to possess power
6. The urge to love (separate and distinct from the desire for sex)
7. The desire for revenge (a characteristic of undeveloped minds)
8. The desire to indulge in egotism

People make use of great power only when urged by one or more of these eight motives. The imaginative forces of the human mind become active when spurred on by the stimulation of well-defined motive! Master salespeople have discovered this. Without this discovery no one could become a master at sales.

What is salesmanship? It is the presentation of an idea, plan or suggestion that gives the prospective purchaser a strong motive for making a purchase. The able salesperson never asks a purchaser to buy without presenting a well-defined motive as to why they should purchase.

Knowledge of merchandise or service offered, in itself, is not sufficient to ensure sales success. The offering must be accompanied by a thorough description of the motive meant to prompt the purchaser to buy. The most effective sales plan is one that appeals to the prospective purchaser through the greatest number of the eight basic motivating forces listed above. The best plan is one that crystallises these motives into a burning desire for the object offered for sale.

The eight basic motives serve not only as the basis of appeal to other minds, where cooperative action from other people is sought, but they serve also as the starting point of action in one's own mind. People of ordinary ability become superhuman when aroused by some outward or inner stimulant that provokes one or more of the eight basic motives for action.

Bring someone face to face with the possibility of death, in a sudden emergency, and he or she will develop physical strength and imaginative strategy that would be impossible under ordinary circumstances.

With the natural desire for sexual contact driving them, people will plan, imagine and indulge in a thousand different amazing things, none of which they'd be able to come up with otherwise.

The desire for financial gain will also lift those of mediocre ability into positions of great power. This desire also causes them to plan, imagine and act in extraordinary ways. The desire for fame and for personal power over others is clearly the chief motivating force in the lives of leaders in every walk of life.

The animalistic desire for revenge often drives people to develop the most intricate and ingenious plans for carrying out their objective.

Love for the opposite sex (and sometimes for the same sex) serves as a mind stimulant leading to almost unbelievable heights of achievement.

The desire for life after death is such a strong motivating force that it not only drives people to both constructive and destructive extremes, but it also develops highly effective leadership ability, evidence of which may be found in the life work of practically all the founders of religions.

And of course the desire to serve the ego as the centre of all society will prompt even the weak to drive themselves towards a lofty goal.

If you would like to achieve great success, then, plant in your mind a strong motive!

Millions of people struggle all the days of their lives with no stronger motive than that of being able to acquire the necessities of life, such as food, shelter and clothing. Now and then someone will step out of the ranks of this great army and demand more than a mere living. He or she will be motivated by the strong desire for fortune, and presto! As if by the hand of magic, his or her financial status changes and action begins to turn into cash.

Power and success are different words for the same

thing. Success is not attained through honesty alone, as some would have us believe. Homeless shelters are filled with people who were, perhaps, honest enough. They failed to accumulate money because they lacked the knowledge of how to acquire and use power!

The Master Mind principle described in this lesson is the medium through which all personal power is applied. For this reason, every known mind stimulant and every basic motive inspiring action in all human endeavour has been mentioned in this chapter.

The Two Faces of Power

We will examine two forms of power in this lesson. One is mental power, and it is acquired through the process of thought. It is expressed through definite plans of action and is the result of organised knowledge. The ability to think, plan and act in a well-organised way is the starting point of all mental power.

The other form of power is physical. It is expressed through natural laws, in the form of electricity, gravity, steam pressure and so on. In this lesson we will analyse both mental and physical power, and explain the relationship between the two.

Knowledge, alone, is not power. Great personal power is acquired only through the harmonious cooperation of a number of people who concentrate their efforts upon some definite plan.

The Nature of Physical Power

The state of advancement known as 'civilisation' is the measure of the knowledge the human race has accumulated. Among the useful knowledge organised and available, humans have discovered and catalogued the 80-plus physical elements that are the building blocks for all material forms in the universe.

Through study, analysis and accurate measurements, science has discovered the 'bigness' of the material side of the universe, as represented by planets, suns and stars, some of which are known to be over one million times as large as the little earth on which we live.

On the other hand, the 'littleness' of the physical forms that constitute the universe has been discovered by reducing physical elements to molecules, atoms, to the electron and way beyond. An electron cannot be seen; it is but a centre of force consisting of a positive or a negative.

MOLECULES, ATOMS, ELECTRONS AND BEYOND

To understand the process through which knowledge is gathered, organised and classified, it seems essential for the student to begin with the smallest and simplest particles of physical matter. These are the A B Cs with which Nature has constructed the entire physical portion of the universe.

The molecule consists of atoms. These are said to be invisible particles of matter that revolve in a continuous circuit at the speed of lightning. What causes them to revolve is gravity and electromagnetism: exactly the same principles with which the earth revolves on its axis. Atoms are said to be made up of electrons, protons and neutrons. As already stated, the electron is nothing but two forms of force. The electron is uniform, of but one class, size and nature. Thus in a grain of sand or a drop of water is duplicated the entire principle upon which the whole universe operates.

How stupendous! You may gather some slight idea of the magnitude of it all the next time you eat a meal by remembering that every article of food you eat, the plate on which you eat it, the tableware and the table itself, are, in final analysis, but a collection of invisible particles.

In the world of physical matter, whether one is looking at the largest star that floats through the heavens or the smallest grain of sand to be found on earth, the object under observation is but an organised collection of molecules, atoms, electrons and smaller particles, revolving at inconceivable speed. Every particle of physical matter is in a continuous state of highly agitated motion. Nothing is ever still, although nearly all physical matter may appear, to the physical eye, to be motionless. There is no 'solid' physical matter. The hardest piece of steel is but an organised mass of revolving molecules. Moreover, the electrons in a piece of steel are of the same nature, but move at different rates of speed, as the electrons in gold, silver, brass or pewter.

The numerous forms of physical matter appear to be different from one another, and they are different, because they are made up of different combinations of atoms. Electrons in those atoms are always the same, and carry a specific negative charge, but their combination with positively charged protons and neutrally charged neutrons produces different forms of matter.

As an illustration, an atom of mercury contains 80 positive charges (protons) in its nucleus, and 80 negative outlying charges (electrons). If the chemist were to expel two of its positive charges, it would instantly become the metal known as platinum. If the chemist then could go a step further and take from it a negative ('planetary') electron, the mercury atom would have lost two positive electrons and one negative; that is, one positive charge on the whole; hence it would retain 79 positive charges on the nucleus and 79 outlying negative electrons, thereby becoming gold! The formula through which this electronic change might be produced has been the object of diligent search by alchemists throughout the ages, as well as chemists of today.

Some of the ablest thinkers have reasoned that the

earth on which we live, and every material particle of the earth, began with two atoms that attached themselves to each other, and through hundreds of millions of years of flight through space, kept contracting and accumulating other atoms until, step by step, the earth was formed. This, they point out, would account for the various and differing stratums of the earth's substances, such as the coal beds, the iron ore deposits, the gold and silver deposits, the copper deposits and so on. They reason that, as the earth whirled through space, it contracted groups of various kinds of nebulae, which it promptly appropriated through the law of magnetic attraction. There is much to be seen, in the earth's surface composition, to support this theory, although there may be no positive evidence of its soundness.

We have referred to these facts concerning the smallest particles of matter because it is a starting point from which we shall undertake to ascertain how to develop and apply the laws of power. It has been noticed that all matter is in a constant state of vibration or motion; that the molecule is made up of rapidly moving particles called atoms, which, in turn, are made up of rapidly moving particles called electrons.

THE VIBRATING PRINCIPLE OF MATTER

In every particle of matter there is an invisible force that causes the atoms to move around one another at an inconceivable rate of speed. Call it vibration. It is believed by some investigators that the rate of speed with which this force (call it whatever you will) moves determines the nature of the physical objects of the universe.

One rate of vibration causes what is known as sound. The human ear can detect only the sound which is produced through vibrations that range from 32,000 to 38,000 per second. As the rate of vibrations per second increases above what we call sound, they begin to manifest themselves in the form of heat. Heat begins with about one and a half million vibrations per second. Still higher up the scale, vibrations begin to register in the form of light. Three million vibrations per second create violet light. Above this number vibration sheds ultraviolet rays (that are invisible to the naked eye) and other invisible radiations. And still higher up the scale, just how high no one at present seems to know, vibrations create the power with which humans think.

It is the belief of this author that the portion of vibration out of which grows all known forms of energy is universal in nature; that the 'fluid' portion of sound is the same as the 'fluid' portion of light, the difference in effect between sound and light being only in rate of vibration; also that the 'fluid' portion of thought is exactly the same as that in sound, heat and light, excepting the number of vibrations per second. Just as there is but one form of physical matter, of which the earth and all the other planets, suns and stars are composed – the electron – so is there but one form of 'fluid' energy that causes all matter to remain in a constant state of rapid motion.

AIR AND ATMOSPHERE

Air is a localised substance that performs, in the main, the service of feeding all animal and plant life with oxygen and nitrogen, without which neither could exist. Nitrogen is one of the chief necessities of plant life, and oxygen one of the mainstays of animal life. Near the top of very high mountains the air becomes very light because it contains but little nitrogen, which is the reason why trees grow smaller on the way up and plant life cannot exist at the highest elevations. On the other hand, the air found in the high altitude consists largely of oxygen, which is the chief reason why tubercular patients used to be sent to the mountains.

What does all this scientific material have to do with you and your goals? You will soon see that it's the very foundation of the philosophy of success that will make reaching those goals possible. Do not become discouraged if all these laboratory facts aren't exactly thrilling to read. If you are seriously engaged in finding out what your available powers are, and how to organise and apply these powers, you must combine determination, persistence and a well-defined desire to gather and organise such knowledge.

Your Mind is a Two-way Radio

Alexander Graham Bell was, of course, one of the world's authorities on the subject of vibration, which is the basis of all mental power and of all thought. The following is as true today as the day the inventor of the telephone wrote it:

Suppose you have the power to make an iron rod vibrate with any desired frequency in a dark room. At first, when vibrating slowly, its movement will be indicated by only one sense, that of touch. As soon as the vibrations increase, a low sound will emanate from it and it will appeal to two senses.

At about 32,000 vibrations to the second the sound will be loud and shrill; but at 40,000 vibrations it will be silent and the movements of the rod will not be perceived by touch. Its movements will be perceived by no ordinary human sense.

From this point up to about one million and a half vibrations per second, we have no sense that can comprehend any effect of the intervening vibrations. After that stage is reached, movement is indicated first by the sense of temperature and then, when the rod becomes red hot, by the sense of sight. At three million vibrations it sheds violet light. Above that it sheds ultraviolet rays and other invisible radiations, some of which can be perceived by instruments and employed by us.

Now it has occurred to me that there must be a great deal to be learned about the effect of those vibrations in the great gap where ordinary human senses are unable to hear, see or feel the movement. The power to send wireless messages by ether vibrations lies in that gap, but the gap is so great that it seems there must be much more. You must make machines practically to supply new senses, as the wireless instruments do.

Can it be said, when you think of that great gap, that there are not many forms of vibrations that may give us results as wonderful as, or even more wonderful than, the wireless waves? It seems to me that in this gap lie the vibrations which we have assumed to be given off by our brain and nerve cells when we think. But then, again, they may be higher up in the scale beyond the vibrations that produce the ultraviolet rays. [Author's note: The last sentence suggests the theory held by this author – WHEN MIND SPEAKS DIRECTLY TO MIND]

Do we need a wire to carry these vibrations? Will they not pass through the ether without a wire, just as the wireless waves do? How will they be perceived by the recipient? Will they hear a series of signals, or will they find that another person's thoughts have entered into their brain?

We may indulge in some speculations based on what we know of the wireless waves, which, as I have said, are all we can recognise of a vast series of vibrations which theoretically must exist. If the thought waves are similar to the wireless waves, they must pass from the brain and flow endlessly around the world and the universe. The body and the skull and other solid obstacles would form no obstruction to their passage, as they pass through the ether which surrounds the molecules of every substance, no matter how solid and dense.

You ask if there would not be constant interference and confusion if other people's thoughts were flowing through our brains and setting up thoughts in them that did not originate with ourselves? How do you know that other people's thoughts are not interfering with yours now? I have noticed a good many phenomena of mind disturbances that I have never been able to explain. For instance, there is the inspiration or the discouragement that a speaker feels in addressing an audience. I have experienced this many times in my life and have never been able to define exactly the physical causes of it.

Many recent scientific discoveries, in my opinion, point to a day, not far distant perhaps, when people will read one another's thoughts, when thoughts will be conveyed directly from brain to brain without the intervention of speech, writing or any of the present known methods of communication. Putting ideas to work is a profitable business, but it makes a slight difference whether the ideas were created by you or by someone else. It is not unreasonable to look forward to a time when we shall see without eyes, hear without ears, and talk without tongues.

Briefly, the hypothesis that mind can communicate directly with mind rests on the theory that thought or vital force is a form of electrical disturbance, that it can be taken up by induction and transmitted to a distance either through a wire or simply through the all-pervading ether, as in the case of wireless telegraph waves. There are many analogies which suggest that thought is of the nature of an electrical disturbance. A nerve which is of the same substance as the brain is an excellent conductor of the electric current. When we first passed an electrical current through the nerves of a dead man, we were shocked and amazed to see him sit up and move. The electrified nerves produced contraction of the muscles very much as in life.

The nerves appear to act upon the muscles very much as the electric current acts upon an electromagnet. The current magnetises a bar of iron placed at right angles to it, and the nerves produce, through the intangible current of vital force that flows through them, contraction of the muscular fibres that are arranged at right angles to them.

It would be possible to cite many reasons why thought and vital force may be regarded as of the same nature as electricity. The electric current is held to be a wave motion of the ether – the hypothetical substance that fills all space and pervades all substances. We believe that there must be ether, because without it the electric current could not pass through a vacuum, or sunlight through space. It is reasonable to believe that only a wave motion of a similar character can produce the phenomena of thought and vital force. We may assume that the brain cells act as a battery and that the current produced flows along the nerves.

But does it end there? Does it not pass out of the body in waves which flow around the world unperceived by our senses, just as the wireless waves passed unperceived before Hertz and others discovered their existence? This author has proved, to his own satisfaction at least, that every human brain is both a broadcasting and a receiving station for vibrations of thought frequency. If this theory should turn out to be a fact, and methods of reasonable control should be established, imagine the part it would play in the gathering, classifying and organising of knowledge. The possibility, much less the probability, of such a reality staggers the mind!

WHOSE THOUGHTS MADE PAINE A GENIUS?

Thomas Paine was one of the great minds of the American Revolutionary period. To him we give credit, more perhaps than to any other one person, for both the beginning and the happy ending of the Revolution. For it was his keen mind that both helped in drawing up the Declaration of Independence and in persuading the signers of that document to translate it into reality.

In speaking of the source of his great storehouse of knowledge, Paine thus described it:

Any person who has made observations on the state of progress of the human mind, by observing his own, cannot but have observed that there are two distinct classes of what are called thoughts: those that we produce in ourselves by reflection and the act of thinking, and those that bolt into the mind of their own accord. I have always made it a rule to treat these voluntary visitors with civility, taking care to examine, as well as I was able, if they were worth entertaining; and it is from them I have acquired almost all the knowledge that I have. As to the learning that any person gains from school education, it serves only like a small capital, to put him in the way of beginning learning for himself afterwards. Every

18

person of learning is finally his own teacher, the
reason for which is that principles, being of a
distinct quality to circumstances, cannot be
impressed upon the memory; their place of mental
residence is the understanding, and they are never
so lasting as when they begin by conception.

In the foregoing words, Paine, the great American
patriot and philosopher, described a phenomenon
which at one time or another is the experience of every
person. Who is so unfortunate as not to have received
positive evidence that thoughts and even complete ideas
will 'pop' into the mind from the outside sources?

What means of conveyance is there for such visitors
except the air? It is the medium of conveyance for all
known forms of vibration such as sound, light and heat.
Why would it not be, also, the medium of conveyance
of the vibration of thought?

EVERY MIND IS CONNECTED

Every mind, or brain, is directly connected with every
other brain. Every thought released by any brain may be
instantly picked up and interpreted by all other brains
that are in rapport with the sending brain. This author is
as sure of this fact as he is that the chemical formula H_2O
will produce water.

It is the belief of this author that every thought

vibration released by any brain is picked up in the atmosphere and kept in motion in circuitous wavelengths. The length of the wave depends on the intensity of the energy used in releasing the thought. These vibrations remain in motion, and are one of the two sources of the thoughts that so often 'pop' into one's mind. The other source is the direct and immediate contact with the brain that is releasing the thought vibration. If this theory is a fact, the boundless space of the whole universe is literally a library containing all the thoughts released by humankind. This is the basis for one of the most important points made in this chapter.

According to scientists, most of the useful knowledge available to the human race has been preserved and accurately recorded in Nature's Bible: the earth. By turning back the pages of this unalterable Bible, we may read the story of the terrific struggle that produced this civilisation. The pages of this Bible are made up of the physical elements of earth and the other planets, and of the atmosphere that contains them. By turning back the pages written on stone and on the surface of this earth, we have uncovered the bones, skeletons, footprints and other unmistakable evidence of the history of animal life through many epochs and eras. The evidence is plain and unmistakable. The great stone pages of Nature's Bible constitute an authentic source of communication between the Creator and humankind. This earth Bible was begun before humans had reached the thinking stage – indeed, before the amoeba stage of development was reached. This Bible is above and beyond the power of humans to alter. Moreover, it tells its story in universal language.

VIBRATIONS, WAVES AND THOUGHTS

Though we take them for granted, we must not fail to see the marvel in the everyday miracles at our disposal. Our ancestors could not have imagined that ordinary vibrations such as made by a human voice hitting a thin metal plate could be converted to sounds emerging from a radio in a distant home. The electric waves that are created from these vibrations move out in all directions at the speed of light: 186,000 miles (300,000 km) per second. Similarly, our television sets pick up radio waves and turn them back into sound and pictures. Our telephones permit vibrating electric signals to flow in an electromagnet inside the receiver, making a steel diaphragm vibrate and emit sound.

These everyday realities – the instantaneous transmission of sound vibrations – make it easier for us to see the transmission of thought vibrations from mind to mind as equally real.

The Master Mind: Two Creating a Mighty Third

We're now ready to look at another way we can gather, classify and organise THE useful knowledge that is essential for success. This is the alliance of two minds, which creates a third. We call that the Master Mind. I first heard the term 'Master Mind' from one of the richest and most powerful men in history: Andrew Carnegie. It's an abstract principle that deals with the effect of one mind upon other minds.

I am among those who believe that the mind is made up of the same energy that fills the universe. But since all minds are not the same, some minds clash the moment they come in contact with each other, because there are varying degrees of affinity and antagonism.

Some minds are so naturally adapted to each other that 'love at first sight' is the inevitable outcome of the contact. Who has not known such an experience? In other cases minds are so antagonistic that violent mutual dislike shows itself at first meeting. These results occur without a word being spoken, and without the slightest signs of any of the usual reasons for love and hate. Whatever the reason, there seems to be an actual chemical reaction, and the resulting vibrations have either a pleasant or unpleasant effect.

The 'meeting of two minds' is an effect that is obvious to even the casual observer. This effect must have a cause like any other, and it resides in the new field created by the meeting, where the two minds are rearranging themselves. Both states of mind are different from what they were prior to their meeting. That this reaction takes place in every instance is a known fact, which gives us a starting point from which we may show what is meant by the term 'Master Mind'.

A Master Mind may be created through the bringing together or blending, in a spirit of perfect harmony, of two or more minds. Out of this harmonious blending, the chemistry of the mind creates a third mind which may be appropriated and used by one or all of the individual minds. This Master Mind will remain available as long as the friendly, harmonious alliance between the individual minds exists. It will disintegrate, and all evidence of its existence disappear, the moment the friendly alliance is broken.

This principle of mind chemistry is the basis and cause of practically all the incidents of 'soul mates' meeting and 'eternal triangles' being formed. Divorce courts, tabloids and scandal aside, these dramatic situations are in fact evidence of one of the greatest of Nature's laws. The entire civilised world knows that the first two or three years of marriage are often marked by much disagreement of a more or less petty nature. These are the years of 'adjustment'. If the marriage survives them, it is more than apt to become a permanent alliance. These facts no experienced married person will deny.

Again we see the 'effect' without understanding the 'cause'.

While there are other contributing causes, this period of adjustment during the early years of marriage takes place because the chemistry of the two minds is slow in blending harmoniously. When first they meet, the mental energies of the two minds are often neither extremely friendly nor antagonistic. Through constant association they adapt themselves, gradually achieving harmony, except in the rare cases where open hostility exists.

It is a well-known fact that after a man and a woman have lived together for 10 to 15 years, they become practically indispensable to each other, even though there may not be the slightest evidence of the state of mind called love. Moreover, this association and sexual relationship not only develops a natural affinity between the two minds, but it actually causes the two people to take on a similar facial expression and to closely resemble each other in many other marked ways. Any competent analyst of human nature can easily go into a crowd of strange people and pick out the wife after having been introduced to her husband. The expression of the eyes, the contour of the faces and the tone of the voices of the people who have long been associated in marriage become similar to a marked degree.

Any experienced public speaker may quickly interpret the manner in which statements from the podium are accepted by the audience, so powerful is the effect of the chemistry of the human mind. Antagonism in the mind of but one person in an audience of one thousand may be readily detected by the speaker who has learned how to 'feel' and register the effects of antagonism. Moreover, the public speaker can make these interpretations without observing, or in any manner being influenced by, the expressions on the faces of those in the audience. An audience may cause such a speaker to rise to great heights of oratory, or heckle the speaker into failure, without making a sound or denoting a single facial expression.

All master salespeople recognise the moment the 'psychological time for closing' has arrived; not by what the prospective buyer says, but from the effect of mind chemistry as interpreted or 'felt'. Words often belie the intentions of those speaking them, but a correct interpretation of the chemistry of the mind leaves no loophole for such a possibility. Everyone practised at sales knows that the majority of buyers have a habit of affecting a negative attitude almost to the very climax of a sale.

Every able lawyer has developed a sixth sense in order to 'feel' his or her way through the most artfully selected words of the clever witness who is lying. Such a lawyer will correctly interpret that which is in the mind of the witness through the chemistry of the mind. Many lawyers have developed this ability without knowing the real source of it; they possess the technique without the scientific understanding upon which it is based. Many salespeople have done the same thing.

One who is gifted in the art of correctly interpreting the chemistry of the minds of others may, figuratively speaking, walk in at the front door of the 'mansion' of a given mind. They may leisurely explore the entire building, noting all its details, and walk out again with a complete picture of the interior of the mental building without the owner knowing that they have entertained a visitor. It will be observed, in the chapter on Accurate Thinking, that this principle may be put to a very practical use (having reference to the principle of the chemistry of the mind).

That's the principle of mind chemistry. We have proven, with the aid of the reader's own everyday experiences and observations, that the moment two minds come within close range of each other, a notice-able mental change takes place in both. Sometimes the change registers as antagonism and at other times as friendliness. Every mind has what might be termed an electric field. The nature of this field varies, depending upon the 'mood' of the individual mind and upon the nature of the chemistry of the mind creating the electric field. It is believed by this author that the normal or natural condition of the chemistry of any individual mind is the combined result of physical heredity and the nature of the thoughts that have dominated that mind.

Every mind is continuously changing, to the extent that the individual's philosophy and general habits of thought change the chemistry of his or her mind. These principles the author believes to be true. That any individual may voluntarily change the chemistry of his or her mind so that it will either attract or repel all with whom it comes in contact is a known fact! To put it another way, anyone may assume a mental attitude that will attract and please others or repel and antagonise them, and this without the aid of words, or facial expression, or other form of bodily movement or demeanour.

Go back, now, to the definition of a Master Mind – a mind that grows out of the blending and coordination of two or more minds, in a spirit of perfect harmony – and you will catch the full significance of the word 'harmony' as it is here used. Two minds will not blend, nor can they be coordinated, unless the element of perfect harmony is present. Therein lies the secret of success or failure for practically all business and social partnerships.

Every sales manager, military commander and leader in all other walks of life understands the necessity of an 'esprit de corps' – a spirit of common understanding and cooperation – in the attainment of success. This mass spirit of harmony of purpose is obtained through discipline, whether voluntary or forced. The nature of this discipline must be such that the individual minds become blended into a Master Mind, by which is meant that the chemistry of the individual minds is modified in such a manner that these minds blend and function as one.

The methods through which this 'blending' process takes place are as numerous as are the individuals engaged in the various forms of leadership. Every leader has his or her own method of coordinating the minds of the followers. One will use force. Another uses persuasion. One will play upon the fear of penalties, while another plays upon rewards, in order to reduce the individual minds of given groups of people to where they may be blended into a unified mind. The student will not have to search deeply into the history of statesmanship, politics, business or finance in order to discover the technique employed by the leaders in these fields in the process of blending the minds of individuals into a harmonious single mind.

The really great leaders of the world, however, seem to have been provided by Nature with such a favourable mind chemistry that it acts as a nucleus of attraction for other minds. Napoleon Bonaparte was a notable example of a man possessing a type of mind so magnetic that it had a very decided tendency to attract all minds with which it came in contact. Soldiers followed Napoleon to certain death without flinching, because of the impelling or attracting nature of his personality, and that personality was nothing more nor less than the chemistry of his mind.

No group of minds can be blended into a Master Mind if one of the individuals of that group possesses an extremely negative, repellent mind. The negative and positive minds will not blend in the sense here described as a Master Mind. Lack of knowledge of this fact has brought many an otherwise able leader to defeat.

Any leader who understands this principle of mind chemistry may temporarily blend the minds of practically any group of people, so that it will represent a mass mind, but the composition will disintegrate almost the very moment the leader's presence is removed from the group. The most successful life insurance sales organisations and other sales forces meet once a week, or more often, for the purpose of merging the individual minds into a Master Mind, which will, for a limited number of days, serve as a stimulus to the individual minds! It may be, and generally is, true that the leaders of these groups do not understand what actually takes place in these meetings, which are usually given over to talks by the leader and other members of the group. While that is going on, the minds of the individuals are 'contacting' and recharging one another.

The brain of a human being may be compared to an electric battery, in that it will become exhausted or run down, causing the owner of it to feel despondent, discouraged and lacking in energy. Who is so fortunate as never to have had such a feeling? When in this depleted condition, the human brain must be recharged, and the manner in which this is done is through contact with a more vital mind or minds. The great leaders understand the necessity of this 'recharging' process, and, moreover, they understand how to accomplish it. This knowledge is the main feature that distinguishes a leader from a follower!

Fortunate is the person who understands this principle sufficiently well to keep his or her brain vitalised or 'recharged' by periodically contacting it with a more vital mind. Sexual contact is one of the most effective of the stimuli through which a mind may be recharged, providing the contact is intelligently made between two people who have genuine affection for each other. Any other sort of sexual relationship is a devitaliser of the mind. At this point it seems appropriate to call attention to the fact that all of the great leaders, whatever their walks of life, have been and are people of highly sexed natures. (The word 'sex' is a decent word. You'll find it in all the dictionaries.)

There is a growing tendency on the part of the best-informed physicians and other health practitioners to accept the theory that all diseases begin when the brain of the individual is in a depleted or devitalised state. Put another way, it is a known fact that a person who has a perfectly vitalised brain is practically, if not entirely, immune from all manner of disease.

Every intelligent health practitioner, of whatever school or type, knows that 'Nature', or the mind, cures disease in every instance where a cure is effected. Medicines, faith, laying on of hands, chiropractic, osteopathy and all other forms of outside stimulant are nothing more than artificial aids to Nature. To state it correctly, they are mere methods of setting the chemistry of the mind into motion so that it readjusts the cells and tissues of the body, revitalises the brain and otherwise causes the human machine to function normally. The most orthodox practitioner should admit the truth of this statement.

What, then, may be the possibilities of the future in the field of mind chemistry? Through the principle of the harmonious blending of minds, perfect health may be enjoyed. Through the aid of this same principle, sufficient power may also be developed to solve the problems of economic necessity that constantly press upon every individual. We may judge the future possibilities of mind chemistry by taking an inventory of its past achievements, keeping in mind the fact that these achievements have been largely the result of accidental discovery and of chance groupings of minds. Is it not strange that nowhere in history do we find a record of one great man who attained his greatness through deceit, trickery and by double-crossing his business associates?

We are approaching the time when the professorate of the universities will teach mind chemistry the same as other subjects are now taught. Meanwhile, study and experimentation in connection with this subject open vistas of possibility for the individual student.

The Mind and Money

That mind chemistry may be appropriately applied to the workaday affairs of the economic and commercial world is a demonstrable fact. Through the blending of two or more minds, in a spirit of perfect harmony, the principle of mind chemistry may be made to develop sufficient power to enable the individuals whose minds have been thus blended to perform seemingly superhuman feats. Power is the force with which people achieve success in any undertaking. Power, in unlimited quantities, may be enjoyed by any group of people. These people must, however, must be wise enough to submerge their own personalities and their own immediate individual interests, in order to blend their minds in a spirit of perfect harmony.

Observe the frequency with which the word 'harmony' appears throughout this introduction! There can be no development of a Master Mind where this element of perfect harmony does not exist. The individual units of one mind will not blend with the individual units of another mind until the two minds have been aroused and warmed, as it were, by a perfect harmony of purpose. The moment two minds begin to take divergent roads of interest, the individual units of each mind separate, and the third element, known as the Master Mind that grew out of the friendly or harmonious alliance, will disintegrate.

We come, now, to the study of some well-known people who have accumulated great power (and also great fortunes) through the application of the Master Mind. Let us begin with three of history's greatest men, known to be men of great achievement in their respective fields of business and professional endeavour. Their names are Henry Ford, Thomas A. Edison and Harvey Firestone.

In his time, Henry Ford was the most financially powerful of the three. I will go further and say that many who studied Ford believed him to be the most powerful man who ever lived at the time. As far as is known, Ford is the only man who ever lived with sufficient power to outwit the money trust of the United States. It was said at the time that Ford gathered money as a child gathered sand on a beach, easier than most people's ability to raise a month's rent. People marvelled at his ability to send out a call and raise a billion dollars within a week.

Edison, as everyone knows, was a philosopher, scientist and inventor. He was also perhaps the keenest Bible student on earth . . . Nature's Bible, that is. He harnessed and combined Mother Nature's wisdom for the good of humankind, more than any person now living or who ever lived. It was he who brought together the point of a needle and a piece of revolving wax in such a way that the vibration of the human voice was first recorded and reproduced.

It was Edison who first harnessed the lightning and made it serve as a light for man's use, through the aid of the incandescent electric light bulb.

It was Edison who gave the world the motion picture.

These are but a few of his outstanding achievements. These modern 'miracles', performed in the bright light of science, transcend all of the 'miracles' described by Jules Verne and others in books of fiction at the time.

Firestone was the moving spirit of the great Firestone Tire company whose industrial achievements in the automotive industry are legendary.

All three men began their careers, business and professional, without capital and with but little schooling of that type usually referred to as 'education'. And all three ended their lives and careers as well-educated people. All three were enormously wealthy and powerful. Now let us inquire into the source of their wealth and power. Thus far we have been dealing only with effect; whereas the true philosopher wishes to understand the 'cause' of a given effect.

Ford, Edison and Firestone were close personal friends for many years. Early in their careers they were in the habit of going away to the woods once a year for a period of rest, meditation and recuperation. Perhaps not even the great men themselves realised that their minds had become blended during those periods of retreat into a Master Mind that was the real source of each man's individual power. This mass mind, a product of the coordinated individual minds of Ford, Edison and Firestone, enabled these men to 'tune in' to forces and sources of knowledge with which most people are totally unfamiliar.

If there is doubt about either the principle or the effects here described, let the student remember that more than half the theory here set forth is based on known facts. For example, it is known that these three men wielded great power. It is known that they were extremely wealthy. It is known that they began without capital and with but little schooling. It is known that they formed periodic mind contacts. It is known that they were harmonious and friendly. It is known that their achievements were so outstanding as to make it impossible to compare them with those of their peers.

There's another major fact connected with the 'cause' of the achievements of Edison, Ford and Firestone of which we may be sure: these achievements are in no way based upon trickery, deceit or any other form of unnatural law. Neither did these men possess secret knowledge of any particular magic. They worked with natural laws, which, for the most part, are well known to all economists and leaders in the field of science, with the possible exception of the law upon which chemistry of the mind is based. Though more study of the power of the mind goes on every year, it's not officially a 'science' in the traditional sense.

The Master Mind, intuitively used to such advantage by Ford, Firestone and Edison, may be created by any group of people who will coordinate their minds in a spirit of perfect harmony. The group may consist of any number from two upwards. Best results appear available from the blending of six or seven minds.

It has been suggested that Jesus Christ discovered how to make use of the principle of mind chemistry, and that His seemingly miraculous performances grew out of the power He developed through the blending of the minds of His 12 disciples. It has been pointed out that, when one of the disciples broke faith (Judas Iscariot), the Master Mind immediately disintegrated and, seen in limited human terms, Jesus then met with the supreme catastrophe of His life.

When two or more people harmonise their minds and produce the effect known as a Master Mind, each person in the group becomes vested with the power to contact with and gather knowledge through the 'subconscious' minds of all the other members of the group. This power becomes immediately noticeable, having the effect of stimulating the mind to a higher rate of vibration, and otherwise evidencing itself in the form of a more vivid imagination and the consciousness of what appears to be a sixth sense. It is through this sixth sense that new ideas will 'flash' into the mind. These ideas take on the nature and form of the subject dominating the mind of the individual. If the entire group has met for the purpose of discussing a given subject, ideas concerning that subject will come pouring into the minds of all present, as if an outside influence were dictating them. The minds of those participating in the Master Mind become as magnets, attracting ideas and thought stimuli of the most highly organised and practical nature – from no one knows where!

The process of mind blending here described as a Master Mind may be likened to the act of one who connects many electric batteries to a single transmission wire, thereby 'stepping up' the power passing over that line by the amount of energy the batteries carry. So it is in the case of blending individual minds into a Master Mind. Each mind, through the principle of mind chemistry, stimulates all the other minds in the group, until the mind energy thus becomes so great that it penetrates and connects with the universal energy, which, in turn, touches every atom of matter in the universe.

Every public speaker has felt the influence of mind chemistry, for it is a well-known fact that as soon as the individual minds of an audience form a rapport (that is, become attuned to the rate of vibration of another mind) with the speaker, there is a noticeable increase in the speaker's enthusiasm, and he or she often rises to heights of oratory that surprise all, including the speaker.

The first five to ten minutes of the average speech are devoted to what is known as 'warming up'. By this is meant the process through which the minds of the speaker and the audience are becoming blended in a spirit of perfect harmony. Every speaker knows what happens when this state of 'perfect harmony' fails to materialise on the part of the audience.

The seemingly supernatural phenomena sometimes occurring in meetings of religious and spiritual groups are the result of the reaction, upon one another, of the minds in the group. These phenomena seldom begin to manifest themselves during the first 10 to 20 minutes after the group is formed, for the reason that this is about the time required for the minds in the group to become harmonised or blended. The 'messages' received by members of such a group probably come from one of two sources, or from both, namely:

1. from the vast storehouse of the subconscious mind of some member of the group, or
2. from the universal storehouse of energy, in which, it is more than probable, all thought vibration is preserved.

It is a known fact that any individual may explore the store of knowledge in another's mind through this principle of mind chemistry, and it seems reasonable to suppose that this power may be extended to include contact with whatever vibrations are available, if there are any.

The theory that all the higher and more refined vibrations, such as thought, are intact and preserved grows out of the known fact that neither matter nor energy (the two known elements of the universe) may be either created or destroyed. It is reasonable to suppose that all such vibrations will survive forever. The lower vibrations, however, probably survive for a natural life span and die out.

All the so-called geniuses probably gained their reputations because, by mere chance or otherwise, they formed alliances with other minds, enabling them to 'step up' their own mind vibrations. They were then enabled to contact the vast Temple of Knowledge, where information is recorded and filed. Moreover, as far as this author has been enabled to ascertain, all of the great geniuses were highly sexed people. The fact that sexual contact is the greatest known mind stimulant lends colour to the theory herein described.

Enquiring further into the source of economic power, as manifested by the achievements of prominent people in the field of business, let us study the case of the Chicago group known as the Big Six. One member of this powerful group was William Wrigley, Jr., whose name is synonymous with chewing gum, and who, 100 years ago, earned the magical sum of more than $15 million a year. There was also the owner of a restaurant chain, an advertising tycoon, the founder of an early forerunner of Federal Express, and the owner of a taxicab company whose name would take on enormous power in the as-yet-unborn field of rental cars. His name was Hertz.

At the time, a reliable financial reporting company estimated the yearly income of these six men at upwards of $25 million, an astounding sum for those years. Analysis of this entire group of six men discloses the fact that, as with the group of three moguls discussed above, not one of them had any special educational advantages. All began without capital or extensive credit. Their financial achievements were due to their own individual plans, and not to any fortunate turn of the wheel of chance.

Many years ago these six men formed a friendly alliance, meeting at stated periods for the purpose of assisting one another with the day-to-day running and furthering of their various industries and businesses. These meetings were strictly for the purpose of cooperating on a give-and-take basis, assisting one another with ideas and suggestions.

There is something about the financial success of this particular group that is well worth comment, study, analysis and even emulation, and that is the fact that they learned how to coordinate their individual minds by blending them in a spirit of perfect harmony, thereby creating a Master Mind that unlocked to each individual of the group doors that are closed to most of the human race.

The United States Steel Corporation has always been one of the strongest and most powerful industrial organisations in the world. The idea out of which this great industrial giant grew was born in the mind of Elbert H. Gary, a more or less commonplace lawyer, who was born and reared in a small Illinois town near Chicago that was later named for him. Gary also surrounded himself with a group whose minds successfully blended in a spirit of perfect harmony, thereby creating the Master Mind that became the moving spirit of the great United States Steel Corporation.

Search where you will, and wherever you find an outstanding success in business, finance, industry, or in any of the professions, you may be sure that underpinning the success is some individual who has applied the principle of mind chemistry through which a Master Mind has been created. These outstanding successes often appear to be the handiwork of but one person, but search closely and the other individuals whose minds have been coordinated with his or hers may be found. Remember that it takes just two or more to operate the principle of mind chemistry that results in a Master Mind.

Power (human power, that is) is simply organised knowledge, expressed through intelligent action! No effort can be said to be organised unless the individuals engaged in the effort coordinate their knowledge and energy in a spirit of perfect harmony. Lack of such harmonious coordination of effort is the main cause of practically every business failure.

An interesting experiment was conducted by this author in collaboration with the students of a well-known college. Each student was requested to write an essay on 'How and Why Henry Ford Became Wealthy'. Each student was required to describe, as a part of his or her essay, what was believed to be the nature of Ford's real assets. The majority of the students gathered financial statements and inventories of the Ford assets and used these as the basis of their estimates of Ford's wealth. Included in these 'sources of Ford's wealth' were such items as cash in banks, raw and finished materials in stock, real estate, buildings and so on. One student, out of the entire group of several hundred, answered as follows (the italics are this author's):

Henry Ford's assets consist, in the main, of two items, viz: (1) Working capital and raw and finished materials; (2) *The knowledge gained from experience by Henry Ford himself, and the cooperation of a well-trained organisation that understands how to apply this knowledge to best advantage from the Ford viewpoint.* It is impossible to estimate, with anything approximating correctness, the actual dollars and cents value of either of these two groups of assets, but it is my opinion that their relative values are:

The organised knowledge of the Ford Organisation –
75 per cent

The value of cash and physical assets of every nature, including raw and finished materials – 25 per cent

This author is of the opinion that this statement was not compiled by the young man whose name was signed to it without the assistance of some very analytical and experienced mind or minds.

Unquestionably the biggest asset that Henry Ford had was his own brain. Next to this would come the brains of his immediate circle of associates, for it was through the coordination of these that the physical assets he controlled were accumulated.

If at the time you had destroyed every plant the Ford Motor Company owned, every piece of machinery, every ton of raw or finished material, every finished car, and every dollar on deposit in any bank, Henry Ford would still have been the most powerful man, economically, on earth. The brains that built the Ford business could duplicate it again in short order. Capital is always available, in unlimited quantities, to such brains as Ford's. Economically, Ford was the most powerful man on earth because he had the keenest and most practical conception of the principle of organised knowledge of any man then on earth, as far as this author has the means of knowing.

Despite Ford's great power and financial success, though, it may be that he blundered often in the application of the principles through which he accumulated this power. There is little doubt that Ford's methods of mind coordination were often crude in the early years, before he gained the wisdom and skill that would come naturally with maturity of years.

Neither can there be much doubt that Ford's application of the principle of mind chemistry was, at least at the start, the result of a chance alliance with other minds, particularly the mind of Edison. It is more than probable that Ford's remarkable insight into the law of Nature was first begun as the result of his friendly alliance with his own wife long before he ever met either Edison or Firestone. Many a man is made by his wife, through application of the Master Mind principle, who never knows the real source of his success. Mrs Ford was a remarkably intelligent woman, and this author has reason to believe that it was her mind, blended with her husband's, that gave him his first real start towards power.

It may be mentioned, without in any way depriving Ford of any honour or glory, that in his earlier days he had to combat the powerful enemies of illiteracy and ignorance to a greater extent than did either Edison or Firestone. Both were gifted by natural heredity with a most fortunate aptitude for acquiring and applying knowledge. Ford had to hew his talent out of the rough, raw timbers of his none-too-favourable heritage.

Within an inconceivably short period of time, Ford mastered three of the most stubborn enemies of humankind and transformed them into assets that became the very foundation of his success. These enemies are: ignorance, illiteracy and poverty! Anyone who can stay the hand of these three savage forces, much less harness and use them to good account, is well worth close study by less-fortunate individuals. The person who has a DEFINITE AIM in mind, and a definite plan for attaining it, has already gone nine-tenths of the way towards success.

We are undoubtedly living in an age of industrial power. The source of all this power is organised effort. A glance at any day's newspaper or attention to any news programme will confirm the vast numbers of corporate, financial or industrial mergers that have brought unprecedented power under one management. One day it is a group of banks; another day it is phone companies; the next week newspaper chains. All are merging for the purpose of developing power through highly organised and coordinated effort.

Knowledge, general in nature and unorganised, is not power; it is only potential power – the material out of which real power may be developed. Any modern library contains an unorganised record of all the valuable knowledge the present civilisation is heir to. But this knowledge is not power because it is not organised.

Every form of energy and every species of animal or plant life must be organised in order to survive. The oversized animals whose bones have filled Nature's bone yard through extinction have left mute but certain evidence that non-organisation means annihilation. From the electron to the largest star in the universe, and every material thing in between, these extremes offer proof positive that one of Nature's first laws is that of organisation. Fortunate is the individual who recognises the importance of this law and makes it his or her business to become familiarised with the various ways this great law works. Those who are astute in business have not only recognised the importance of the law of organised effort, but have also made this law the warp and woof of their power.

Without any knowledge whatsoever of the principle of mind chemistry, many have accumulated great power by merely organising the knowledge they possessed. The majority of all who have discovered the principle of mind chemistry and developed that principle into a Master Mind have stumbled upon this knowledge by the merest of accidents, often failing to recognise the real nature of their discovery or understand the source of their power.

This author is of the opinion that all living persons

currently making conscious use of the principle of mind chemistry in developing power through the blending of minds may be counted on the fingers of two hands, with perhaps several fingers left to spare. If this estimate is even approximately true, the student will readily see that there is but slight danger of the field of mind chemistry practice becoming overcrowded.

It is a well-known fact that one of the most difficult tasks any business person must perform is that of inducing associates to coordinate their efforts in a spirit of harmony. To induce continuous cooperation between a group of workers in any undertaking is next to impossible. Only the most efficient leaders can accomplish this highly desired object, but once in a great while such a leader will rise above the horizon in the field of industry, business or finance, and then the world hears of a Henry Ford, Thomas A. Edison or John D. Rockefeller.

Power and success are synonymous terms! One grows out of the other. Therefore, any person with the knowledge and the ability to develop power through the harmonious coordination of individuals may be successful in any reasonable undertaking. It must not be presumed, though, that a Master Mind will immediately spring, mushroom fashion, out of every group of minds that makes a pretence of coordination in a spirit of harmony! Harmony, in the real sense of the meaning of the word, is as rare among groups of people as is genuine Christianity among those who proclaim themselves Christians. Harmony is the nucleus around which the state of mind known as the Master Mind must be developed. Without this element of harmony there can be no Master Mind, a truth which cannot be repeated too often.

When President Woodrow Wilson proposed the League of Nations, the precursor to the United Nations, he had in mind the development of a Master Mind, a blending of international minds. Wilson's conception was the most far-reaching humanitarian idea ever created in the mind of man at the time, because it dealt with a principle that embraces sufficient power to establish a real Brotherhood of Man on earth.

The greatest future unity of minds will be measured largely by the time required for the great universities and nonsectarian institutions of learning to supplant ignorance and superstition with understanding and wisdom. This time is rapidly approaching.

The Psychology of the Revival Meeting

The old religious orgy known as the 'revival' offers a favourable opportunity to study the principle of mind chemistry known as Master Mind. It will be observed that music plays no small part in bringing about the harmony essential to the blending of a group of minds in a revival meeting. Without music, the revival meeting would be a tame affair.

During revival services the leader of the meeting has no difficulty in creating harmony in the minds of his devotees, but it is a well-known fact that this state of harmony lasts no longer than the presence of the leader, after which the Master Mind he has temporarily created disintegrates. By arousing the emotional nature of his followers, the revivalist has no difficulty, under the proper stage setting and with the embellishment of the right sort of music, in creating a Master Mind that becomes noticeable to all who come in contact with it. The very air becomes charged with a positive, pleasing influence that changes the entire chemistry of all minds present. The revivalist calls this energy the 'Spirit of the Lord'.

This author, through experiments conducted with a group of scientific investigators and laypeople who were unaware of the nature of the experiment, has created the same state of mind and the same positive atmosphere without calling it the 'Spirit of the Lord'. On many occasions this author has witnessed the creation of the same positive atmosphere in a group of men and women engaged in the business of salesmanship, without calling it the 'Spirit of the Lord'.

The author helped conduct a school of salesmanship for Harrison Parker, founder of the Cooperative Society of Chicago. By the use of the same principle of mind chemistry that the revivalist calls the 'Spirit of the Lord', he transformed the nature of a group of 3,000 men and women (all of them were without former sales experience). So much so that they sold more than ten million dollars' worth of securities in less than nine months, and earned more than one million dollars for themselves, at a time when people were earning only a fraction of that amount.

It was found that the average person who joined this school would reach the zenith of his or her selling power within one week, after which it was necessary to revitalise the individual's brain through a group sales meeting. These sales meetings were conducted on very much the same order as the modern revival meetings, with much the same stage equipment, including music and high-powered speakers that exhorted the sales-people in very much the revival manner.

Call it psychology, mind chemistry or anything you please (they are all based upon the same principle), there is nothing more certain than the fact that wherever a group of minds are brought into contact in a spirit of perfect harmony, each mind in the group becomes immediately supplemented and reinforced by a noticeable energy called a Master Mind. For all this writer professes to know, this uncharted energy may be the 'Spirit of the Lord', but it operates just as favourably when called by any other name.

The human brain and nervous system constitute a

piece of intricate machinery which few, if any, understand. When controlled and properly directed, this piece of machinery can be made to perform wonders of achievement and, if not controlled, it will perform in quite another fantastic manner, as may be seen by examining the inmates of any insane asylum.

The human brain has a direct connection with a continuous influx of energy, from which humans derive their power to think. The brain receives this energy, mixes it with the energy created by the food taken into the body, and distributes it to every portion of the body through the aid of the blood and the nervous system. It thus becomes what we call life. From what source this outside energy comes, no one seems to know. All we know about it is that we must have it or die. It seems reasonable to presume that this energy flows into the body, along with the oxygen from the air, as we breathe.

Every normal human body possesses a first-class chemical laboratory and a stock of chemicals sufficient to carry on the business of breaking up, assimilating, and properly mixing and compounding the food we take into the body, preparatory to distributing it to wherever it is needed as a body-builder. Ample tests have been made, both with man and beast, to prove that the energy known as the mind plays an important part in the chemical operation of compounding and transforming food into the required substances to build and keep the body in repair. It is known that worry, excitement or fear will interfere with the digestive process, and in extreme cases stop this process altogether, resulting in illness or death. It is obvious, then, that the mind enters into the chemistry of food digestion and distribution.

It is believed by many eminent authorities, although it may never have been scientifically proven, that the energy known as thought may become contaminated with negative units to such an extent that the whole nervous system is thrown out of working order, digestion is interfered with, and various and sundry forms of disease manifest themselves. Such disturbed minds produce financial difficulties and unrequited love affairs, among other things. A negative environment, for instance where some member of the family is constantly nagging, will interfere with the chemistry of the mind to such an extent that an individual will lose ambition and gradually sink into oblivion. This is the basis of the old saying that one's spouse may either 'make' or 'break' the other.

Certain food combinations will, if taken into the stomach, result in indigestion, violent pain and even death. Good health depends, in part at least, upon a food combination that 'harmonises'. But this harmony of food combination is not sufficient to ensure good health. There must also be harmony between the units of energy that make up the mind. Harmony is one of Nature's laws, without which there can be no such thing as organised energy, or life in any form whatsoever.

The health of the body as well as the mind is literally built upon the principle of harmony! The energy known as life begins to disintegrate and death approaches when the organs of the body stop working in harmony. The moment harmony ceases at the source of any form of organised energy (power), units of that energy are thrown into a chaotic state of disorder and the power is rendered neutral or passive.

Harmony is also the nucleus around which the principle of mind chemistry known as a Master Mind develops power. Destroy this harmony and you destroy the power growing out of the coordinated effort of a group of individual minds. This truth has been stated, restated and presented in every manner that the author could conceive, with unending repetition. For unless the student grasps this principle and learns to apply it, this treatise on the Master Mind is useless.

Success in life, no matter what one may call success, is very largely a matter of adaptation so that there is harmony between the individual and the environment. The palace of a king comes to resemble a hovel of a peasant if harmony does not abound within its walls. Conversely stated, the hut of a peasant may be made to yield more happiness than that of the mansion of the rich man, if harmony obtains in the former and not in the latter.

Without perfect harmony the science of astronomy would be as useless as a set of old bones because the stars and planets would clash with one another and all would be in a state of chaos and disorder.

Without the law of harmony the blood might deposit the food meant to grow fingernails on the scalp, where hair is supposed to grow. That horny growth might easily be mistaken by the superstitious to signify man's relationship to a certain imaginary gentleman with horns, often referred to by the more primitive type.

Without the law of harmony there can be no organisation of knowledge, for what, may one ask, is organised knowledge except the harmony of facts and truths and natural laws?

The moment discord begins to creep in at the front door, harmony edges out at the back door, so to speak, whether the application is made to a business partnership or the orderly movement of the planets of the heavens.

If the student has the impression that the author is laying undue stress upon the importance of harmony, let it be remembered that lack of harmony is the first and often the last and only cause of failure!

There can be no poetry, nor music, nor oratory worthy of notice without the presence of harmony.

Good architecture is largely a matter of harmony. Without harmony a house is nothing but a mass of building material, more or less a monstrosity.

Sound business management plants the very sinews of its existence in harmony.

Every well-dressed man or woman is a living picture and a moving example of harmony.

With all these workaday illustrations of the importance of harmony in the affairs of the world, not to say in the operation of the entire universe, how could any intelligent person leave harmony out of their Definite Aim in life? You might as well have no Definite Aim at all if you omit harmony as the chief stone of its foundation.

The human body is a complex organisation of organs, glands, blood vessels, nerves, brain cells, muscles and so on. The mind energy that stimulates to action and coordinates the efforts of the component parts of the body is also a plurality of ever-varying and changing energies. From birth until death there is a continuous struggle, often assuming the nature of open combat, between the forces of the mind. For example, the lifelong struggle between the motivating forces and desires of the human mind that take place between the impulses of right and wrong are well known.

Every human being possesses at least two distinct mind powers or personalities, and as many as six distinct personalities have been discovered in one person. One of our most delicate tasks is that of harmonising these mind forces so that they may be organised and directed towards the orderly attainment of a given objective. Without this element of harmony no individual can become an accurate thinker.

It is no wonder that leaders in business and industrial enterprises, as well as those in other fields of endeavour, find it so difficult to organise groups of people so they will function without friction in the attainment of a given objective. Each individual human being possesses forces, within themselves, that are hard to harmonise, even when the individual is placed in the environment most favourable to harmony. If the chemistry of the individual's mind is such that the units of their mind cannot be easily harmonised, think how much more difficult it must be to harmonise a group of minds so they will function as one, in an orderly manner, through what is known as a Master Mind.

The leader who successfully develops and directs the energies of a Master Mind must possess tact, patience, persistence, self-confidence, intimate knowledge of mind chemistry and the ability to adapt themselves (in a state of perfect poise and harmony) to quickly changing circumstances without showing the least sign of annoyance.

How many are there who can measure up to this requirement?

The successful leader must possess the ability to change the colour of their mind, chameleon-like, to fit every circumstance that arises in connection with the object of leadership. Moreover, such a leader must possess the ability to change from one mood to another without showing the slightest signs of anger or lack of self-control. The successful leader must understand the 17 Laws of Success and be able to put into practice any combination of these laws whenever occasion demands.

Without this ability no leader can be powerful, and without power no leader can long endure.

The Real Meaning of Education

There has long been a general misconception of the meaning of the word 'educate'. The dictionaries have not aided in the elimination of this misunderstanding because they have defined the word 'educate' as an act of imparting knowledge. Actually, the word educate has its roots in the Latin word *educo*, which means to develop from within; to educe; to draw out; to grow through the law of use.

Nature hates idleness in all its forms. She gives continuous life only to those elements which are in use. Tie up an arm, or any other portion of the body, taking it out of use, and the idle part will soon atrophy and become lifeless. Reverse the order, give an arm more than normal use, such as that engaged in by the blacksmith who wields a heavy hammer all day long, and that arm (developed from within) grows strong.

Power grows out of organised knowledge, but, mind you, it 'grows out of it' through application and use! Someone may become a walking encyclopedia of knowledge without possessing any power. This knowledge becomes power only to the extent that it is organised, classified and put into action. Some of the best-educated people the world has known possessed much less general knowledge than some who have been known as fools, the difference between the two being that the former put what knowledge they possessed into use, while the latter made no such application.

An 'educated' person is one who knows how to acquire everything needed in the attainment of their main purpose in life without violating the rights of others. It might be a surprise to many of the so-called learned to know that they come nowhere near qualification as educated. It might also be a great surprise to many who believe they suffer from lack of 'learning' to know that they are well 'educated'.

The successful lawyer is not necessarily the one who memorises the greatest number of legal principles. On the contrary, the successful lawyer is the one who knows where to find a principle of law, as well as a variety of opinions supporting that principle. In other words, the successful lawyer is the one who knows where to find the law when needed.

This principle applies, with equal force, to the affairs of industry and business. Henry Ford had little elementary schooling, yet he was one of the best-'educated' men in the world. He seemed to have acquired such an ability to combine natural and economic laws, to say nothing of the minds of people, that he attained the power to get anything of a material nature he wanted.

During World War II, Henry Ford brought a suit against the *Chicago Tribune*, charging that newspaper with libellous statements concerning him. One of these was that Ford was an 'ignoramus', an ignorant pacifist, and so on. When the suit came up for trial, the attorneys for the *Tribune* undertook to prove, by interrogating Ford himself, that their statement was true; that he was ignorant. With this aim in view they cross-examined him in the courtroom on all manner of subjects.

One question they asked was: 'How many soldiers did the British send over to subdue the rebellion in the Colonies in 1776?'

With a dry grin on his face Ford nonchalantly replied: 'I do not know just how many, but I have heard that it was a lot more than ever went back.'

The response was loud laughter from court officers, jury, courtroom spectators, and even from the frustrated lawyer who had asked the question. This line of interrogation was continued for an hour or more, with Ford remaining perfectly calm. Finally, however, he had permitted the smart aleck lawyers to play with him until he was tired of it. Then, in reply to a question that was particularly obnoxious and insulting, Ford straightened himself up, pointed his finger at the questioning lawyer, and replied: 'If I should really wish to answer the foolish questions you have just asked, or any of the others you have been asking, let me remind you that I have a row of buttons hanging over my desk. By placing my finger on the right button, I could call in any number of people who could give me the correct answer to all the questions you have asked and to many that you have not the intelligence to either ask or answer. Now, will you kindly tell me why I should bother about filling my mind with a lot of useless details in order to answer every fool question that anyone may ask, when I have able people all about me who can supply me with all the facts I want when I call for them?'

This answer is quoted from memory, but it substantially relates Ford's response. There was silence in the courtroom. The questioning attorney's jaw dropped and his eyes opened wide; the judge leaned forward from the bench and gazed in Mr Ford's direction; many of the jury awoke and looked around as if they had heard an explosion, which they actually had.

Ford's reply knocked the questioner cold.

Up to the time of that reply, the lawyer had been enjoying considerable fun at what he believed to be Ford's expense, by adroitly displaying his sample case of general knowledge and comparing it with what he inferred to be Ford's widespread ignorance. But that answer spoiled the lawyer's fun! It also proved once more (to all who had the intelligence to accept the proof) that true education means mind development, not merely the gathering and classifying of knowledge. Ford could not, in all probability, have named the capitals of all the States, but he could have, and in fact had, gathered the capital with which to turn many wheels within every state in the Union.

Education – let us not forget this – consists of the power to get everything one needs without violating the rights of others. Ford falls well within that definition. There were many men of 'learning' who could easily have entangled Ford, theoretically, with a maze of questions he was unable to answer. But Ford could also have waged a battle in industry or finance that would have exterminated those same men, with all of their abstract knowledge and wisdom.

Ford probably could not have gone into his chemical laboratory and separated water into its component atoms of hydrogen and oxygen and then recombine these atoms in their former order, but he knew how to surround himself with chemists who could have done this for him. Someone who can intelligently use the knowledge possessed by another is as much or more a person of education as the person who merely has the knowledge but does not know what to do with it.

Education consists of doing – not merely of KNOWING!

The Relationship between Sex and Genius

The sex drive is, by far, the most powerful of the eight basic motivating forces that stimulate the mind to action. Because of the importance of this subject, it has been reserved as the closing section of the first of the 17 factors constituting the Law of Success.

The part that sexual urge plays in the achievement of outstanding success was first discovered by the author in his studies of the biographies of great leaders, and in his analysis of men and women of the present age who have risen high in their chosen fields of endeavour. Most people are unpardonably ignorant when it comes to the subject of sex. It's no wonder, since sexual desire has been slandered and burlesqued by the ignorant and the vulgar for so long. Men and women who are known to be blessed with highly sexed natures are often looked upon with suspicion, though it's often secretly accompanied by envy.

During the early years of research, when this philosophy was in the embryonic stage, the author made the discovery that every great leader in art and music, in literature and statesmanship, and in practically every other walk of life, was a highly sexed person. Among the group whose biographies were carefully studied, let us list the following as members of that group:

Napoleon Bonaparte
Shakespeare
George Washington
Abraham Lincoln
Ralph Waldo Emerson
Robert Burns
Thomas Jefferson
Oscar Wilde
Woodrow Wilson
Stanford White
Enrico Caruso

Sexual urge is the highest and most refined form of human emotion. It 'steps up' the rate of vibration of the mind as no other emotion can, and causes the imaginative faculties of the brain to function at the level of genius. Far from being something of which one should be ashamed, a highly sexed nature is a blessing of which one should feel proud.

Sex as a Source of Genius

To be highly sexed is not sufficient, in itself, to produce a genius. Only those who understand the nature of the sexual urge, and who know how to transmute this powerful emotion into other channels of action than that of sexual contact, rise to the status of a genius. The sexual energy is a driving force compared to which all other motivating forces must take second place at best. A mind that has been aroused through intense sexual desire becomes receptive to the impulse of ideas that 'flash' into the mind from outside sources. This is what is ordinarily known as inspiration.

It is the belief of this author – a belief with considerable evidence to back it – that all so-called 'revelations', of whatever nature, from religion to art, are induced by an intense desire for sexual contact. All so-called 'magnetic' people are highly sexed. People who are brilliant, charming, versatile and accomplished are generally highly sexed. Prove this for yourself by analysing those whom you know to be highly sexed.

Destroy the capacity for strong sexual desire and you have removed all that is powerful about a human being. If you wish proof of this, observe what happens to the 'spirited' stallion or any other male animal, such as a bull or a hog, after it has been altered sexually. The moment sexual urge has been destroyed in any animal, from humans down to the lowest forms of animal life, the capacity for dominating action goes with it. This is a statement of biological fact too well known to be disputed. Moreover, it is a significant and important fact.

The Therapeutic Value of Sex

It is a fact well known to scientists, although not generally known to the layperson, that sexual desire has a therapeutic value not attributed to any other human emotion. This fact may be easily verified, however, by observing the physical state of the body following sexual contact between two people who have an affinity and are properly mated. The physical body becomes relaxed and calm. Relaxation, superinduced in this manner, provides the nervous system with a most favourable opportunity to balance and distribute the nervous energy of the body to all the organs. Properly distributed nervous energy is the force that maintains a healthy body. Also, nervous energy, properly distributed through relaxation, eliminates the cause of physical ailments.

These briefly stated facts are not merely the author's opinion. They have been gleaned from many decades of careful research collaborations of some of the most eminent scientists known to the past and present generations. One was a well-known physician who was bold enough to admit that he had often recommended a change in sexual partners for patients who were suffering from hypochondria, which had the desired effect – one that he feels would not have been possible through any other prescription. This physician went even further by predicting that the time was not far distant when this form of therapy would be more generally understood and used. The suggestion is here offered for what it may be worth, without comment from the author of this philosophy, other than the statement that most of the human race is still woefully ignorant of the possibilities of sexual desire and activity, not only in connection with the maintenance of health, but also in connection with the creation of genius.

The significance of that fact impressed the author when he made the discovery that practically every great leader whom he studied at close range was largely inspired by a powerful sexual connection. In the case of some influential men, the partner is a wife of whom the public hears but little. In a few cases the source of inspiration has been traced to the 'other woman'. In either case, a great, enduring love is a sufficient motive to drive even a mediocre person to unbelievable heights of achievement, a statement of fact which should be kept in mind by all such spouses, partners and lovers.

Sexual desire, then, the stuff of songs and dreams, is the most effective known way to energise a mind to the level of Master Mind!

Ten Reasons Why the Mind Moves to Greatness

A mind stimulant is any influence that will, temporarily or permanently, 'step up' the rate of vibration of the brain. All great achievements are the result of one form or another of such stimuli. People are often surprised by learning what some of these stimuli are. Here these 'mind movers' are listed, in order of what the author considers to be their importance:

1. Sexual contact between two people who are motivated by a genuine feeling of love.
2. Love, not necessarily accompanied by sexual contact.
3. A burning desire for fame, power and financial gain.
4. To a highly emotional person, music is a mighty stimulant.
5. Friendship, between either those of the same sex or the opposite sex, provided it is accompanied by a desire to be mutually helpful in making progress with some definite undertaking or calling.
6. A Master Mind alliance between two or more people who ally themselves, mentally, for the purpose of mutual help, in a spirit of unselfishness.
7. Mutual suffering, such as that experienced by people who are unjustly persecuted, through racial, religious and economic differences of opinion.
8. Autosuggestion. An individual may step up his or her own mind through constant self-suggestion backed by a definite motive. (Perhaps this source

of mind stimulation should have been placed nearer the top of the list.)

9. Suggestion. The influence of outside suggestion may lift one to great heights of achievement. If negatively used, it can dash one to the bottomless pit of failure and destruction.

10. Narcotics and alcohol. Although these are known to be sources of mind stimulation, their effects are totally destructive, leading finally to negation of all the other nine sources of stimulation.

Here you have a brief description of all the major sources of mind stimulation. Through these sources of stimulation one may partake of the stuff of genius by communing, temporarily, with Infinite Intelligence. Take or leave that plain and simple statement, just as you please! The statement is made as a positive fact because this author has had the privilege of helping to raise scores of mediocre men and women out of mediocrity into states of mind that placed them squarely in the category of genius. Some have been able to remain in this exalted state, while others have relapsed to their former mediocre status, either temporarily or permanently.

The author personally interviewed and analysed an average of a dozen men and women every day for the purpose of helping them discover the most suitable source of mind stimulation and the most profitable outlet for the talent they displayed through moving their minds in these ways. On many scores of occasions the author had the experience of seeing a client create some useful invention, or some unique plan of rendering useful service, right in the midst of the analysis.

Perhaps these analyses also produced an inadvertent Master Mind side-effect! One such story took place when a client named Gundelach came to see me with his wife. Not 30 minutes into the analysis, he conceived an idea for a new style of interlocking brick suitable for building public roads, an idea that contained the clear possibility of rendering useful service, to say nothing of making a huge fortune for himself. Perhaps it would be more correct to say that the three of us – he and his wife and the author – conceived the idea simultaneously.

Intemperance and Addiction Move the Mind . . . to Failure

Of the 10 stimulants described above, only nine are safe for use, and even these cannot be used excessively. The intemperate use of alcohol and narcotics as mind stimulants is condemned without exception on the grounds that such use eventually destroys the normal functioning power of the brain. While it is true that some of the greatest literary geniuses of the past used alcohol as a mind stimulant, albeit with temporary success, it is equally true that such use generally became an excess that destroyed them. Two writers of the past who are considered classics, Edgar Allan Poe and Robert Burns, both used alcohol as a mind stimulant, with telling effects, but both were finally destroyed through excessive use of this form of stimulant.

Sex is the most powerful of all the mind stimulants, but this, too, may be used to excess with just as damaging effects as the excessive use of alcohol or narcotics. Excessive eating may be just as damaging as any other form of excess, and in many thousands of cases this form of indulgence destroys all possibility of great achievement.

One of the 17 factors of the Law of Success is that of self-control. Later, when we reach that subject, we will expand on the idea that self-control is a balance wheel guarding the individual against excesses of every nature whatsoever. The three major excesses that are destroying people throughout the world today are: excessive and addictive drinking and drug use, eating and sexual behaviour. One is just as fatal to success as either of the other two.

Why Most Succeed After 40

One prominent theory explaining why the majority of strivers don't reach success in their chosen work until the age of 40 points to the extraordinary amount of energy spent on sexual activity in the earlier years. The word 'dissipated' is often used to describe this phenomenon, since such energy is scattered and spread thinly. The average young male, to use him as an example, does not learn that the sexual urge can be useful in areas other than sexual contact itself until he has reached the age of 40 to 45 years. Up to this age the life of the average male (in which classification the majority of all males may be properly placed) is just one long, continuous orgy of sexual intercourse, through which all his finer and more powerful emotions are sown wildly to the four winds. This is not merely the opinion of this author; it is a statement of fact based upon careful analysis of over 20,000 people. Intelligent study of 20,000 people gives a very accurate cross-section classification of the entire human race.

Between overeating and overindulgence in sexual contact, the average man has but little energy left for other uses until he has passed the age of 40. In altogether too many instances, men never gain mastery of themselves at all in these two areas of weakness. A sad statement of fact is that the majority of men do not look upon overindulgence in eating and in sexual contact as being dangerous excesses that destroy their chances of success in life. There is no argument over the detrimental effects of excessive use of alcohol and narcotics, as everyone knows that such overindulgence is fatal to success, but not everyone knows that excesses in sexual contact and in eating can be just as ruinous.

The desire for sexual contact is the strongest, most powerful and most impelling of all human desires. It's for this very reason that it may be harnessed and transmuted into channels other than that of sexual contact in a manner that will raise one to great heights of genius. On the other hand, this powerful urge, if not controlled and so transmuted, may, and often does, lower man to the level of an ordinary beast.

In closing this chapter, may the author not offer a word of reply to those who may feel that even the very brief reference here made to the subject of sex might be harmful to young men and women? The reply is this: ignorance of the subject of sex, due to lack of free discussion of the subject by those who really understand it, has resulted in destructive use of the sexual drive all through the ages. Moreover, if anyone should feel that this brief reference might hurt the morals of the young people of this generation, let that person keep in mind the fact that most young people get their sex education from less commendable sources than a book of this nature, and such education is generally accompanied by interpretations of the power of sex which in no way relate the subjects of sex and genius. These sources of sex information in no manner even suggest that there is such a possibility as the transmutation of sex power into art and literary works of the most commendable order, as well as into business leadership and a multitude of other constructive forms of helpful service. This is an age of frank discussion of the great mysteries of life, among which the subject of sex may be properly classified. Finally, the urge of sex is biological in nature and it cannot be suppressed through silence! In truth, the emotion of sexual urge is the finest of all human emotions, and the sexual relationship the most beautiful of all relationships. Why, then, cast the slurring innuendo that the sexual relationship is something ugly and vulgar by trying to shroud the subject in a dark background of silence?

This ends the subject of the Master Mind. We pass next to the discussion of the second of the 17 factors of the Law of Success, with both apology and regret that this lack of space forbids us to discuss the remaining 16 subjects as extensively as we have covered the subject of the Master Mind.

CHAPTER 2

THE IMPORTANCE OF A DEFINITE AIM

To be successful in any sort of endeavour you must have a definite goal towards which to work. You must have definite plans for attaining this goal. Nothing worthwhile is ever accomplished without a definite plan of procedure that is systematically and continuously followed out day by day. Without a Definite Chief Aim, the other 16 Laws of Success would be useless. For how could one hope to succeed, or how could one know when success had been reached, if the nature of the accomplishment – the goal – had never been determined?

During the past 20-odd years the author has analysed more than 20,000 people from nearly all walks of life. Startling as it may be, 95 per cent of these people were failures. By this is meant that they were barely making enough on which to exist, and some of them were not even doing this well. The other 5 per cent were successful, meaning that they were making enough for all their needs and saving money for the sake of ultimate financial independence.

Now the significant thing about this discovery was that the 5 per cent who were succeeding had a Definite Chief Aim and also a plan for attaining that aim. In other words, those who knew what they wanted, and had a plan for getting it, were succeeding, while those who did not know what they wanted were getting just that – nothing!

If sales is the game, or a steady flow of paying customers is the aim, clear and definite methods of handling customers that will cause them to return and return must be built into a plan. The plan may be one thing, or it may be something else, but in the main it should be distinctive and of such a nature that it will impress itself upon the minds of patrons in a favourable manner. Anyone can hand out merchandise to those who come, voluntarily, and ask for it, but not every-one has acquired the art of delivering, along with the merchandise, that unseen 'something' that causes the customer to repeatedly come back for more. Here is where the necessity of a definite aim and a definite plan for attaining it enters.

In certain neighbourhoods, car repair shops are as common as convenience stores. There may be little difference between the quality received at one and that received at another. Despite this fact, however, there are car owners who will drive miles out of their way to get their car serviced at a favourite garage.

Now, the question arises, 'What causes these people to do this?'

And the answer is, 'People trade at businesses where they are served by those who cultivate them.' What is meant by 'cultivate them'? How do you cultivate a plant? Not by doing only the essentials, such as watering. You 'deadhead' it, removing dead or dying parts; you are attentive to the season, giving it extra food because the calendar suggests it. You notice if it has bugs and you remove them. Any good business owner is such a gardener. One who knows your car will notice when the tyres are balding or the belts fraying, when the antifreeze needs adding to, or the right-turn signal light has blown. In these and scores of other ways, a good business owner impresses the customer with the fact that this is personal service, and can be trusted. All this does not 'just happen'. There is a definite plan and also a definite purpose in doing it, and that purpose is to bring motorists back and back. This is a brief statement of what is meant by a Definite Chief Aim.

Let us now go a bit deeper into the study of the psychological principle upon which the law of a Definite Chief Aim is based. Careful study of more than 100 leaders in practically all walks of life has disclosed the fact that every one of them worked with a Definite Chief Aim and also a definite plan for its attainment.

The human mind is something like a magnet in that it will attract the counterparts of the dominating thoughts held in the mind, and especially those which constitute a Definite Chief Aim or purpose. For example, if someone establishes, as a Definite Chief Aim, and as a daily working purpose, the adding of say 100 new customers who will regularly purchase a given merchandise or service, immediately that aim or purpose becomes a dominating influence that will drive the business owner to do everything necessary to secure these additional customers.

Manufacturers of cars and other lines of merchandise often establish what they call 'quotas', covering the number of cars or the amount of merchandise that must be sold in each territory. These 'quotas', when definitely established, constitute a Definite Chief Aim towards which all who are engaged in the distribution of the cars or merchandise direct their efforts. Seldom does anyone fail to make the established quotas, but it is a well-known fact that had there been no 'quotas' the actual sales would have been far less than they were with them. In other words, to achieve success in selling or in practically any other line of endeavour, one must set up a mark at which to shoot, so to speak, and without this target there will be slim results.

There is one point upon which brain researchers, physicists, psychologists, psychiatrists, counsellors and educators agree. Simply put, it is this: there is a strong connection between the events of your life and your thoughts and beliefs. Therefore, anybody with a definite purpose, and with full faith in his or her ability to realise that purpose, cannot be permanently defeated. There may be a temporary defeat – perhaps many such defeats – but failure, never!

There is one sure way to avoid criticism: be nothing, do nothing! Get a job washing dishes and kill off your priceless ambition. The formula always works. Should you choose, instead, to go the Success route, your first step is to know where you are going, how you intend to travel and when you intend to get there, which is only another way of saying that you must decide upon a Definite Chief Aim. This aim must be written out in clear language so as to be understood by you before it can be understood by any other person. If there is anything 'hazy' about your aim, it is not definite. A successful leader once stated that nine-tenths of success in any undertaking lay in knowing what was wanted. This is true.

The moment you write out a statement of your chief aim, you have planted an image of that aim firmly in your subconscious mind. Through some process that even the most enlightened scientists have not yet discovered, Nature causes your subconscious mind to use that chief aim as a pattern or blueprint guiding the major portion of your thoughts, ideas and efforts towards the attainment of your objective.

This is a strange, abstract truth – something that cannot be weighed or even meditated upon – but it is a truth nevertheless! You will be taken further into the mysteries of this strange law when you reach the law of imagination and other laws, further on.

CHAPTER 3

SELF-CONFIDENCE

The third of the 17 Laws of Success is self-confidence. This term is self-explanatory – it means that to achieve success you must believe in yourself. However, this does not mean that you have no limitations. It means that you are to take an inventory of yourself, find out what qualities you have that are strong and useful, and then organise these qualities into a definite plan of action with which to attain the object of your Definite Chief Aim.

In all the languages of the world there is no one word that carries the same or even approximately the same meaning as the word 'faith'. This does not necessarily refer to faith in a Higher Power, yet if there are any such things as 'miracles', they are performed only with the aid of super-faith. The doubting type of mind is not a creative mind. Search where and how you may, and you will not discover one single record of great achievement, in any line of endeavour, that was not conceived in imagination and brought into reality through faith!

To succeed, you must have faith in your own ability to do whatever you make up your mind to do. Also, you must cultivate the habit of faith in those who are associated with you, whether they are in a position of authority over you, or you over them. The psychological reason for this will be covered thoroughly and plainly in the law on Cooperation, further on.

Doubters are not builders! Had Columbus lacked self-confidence and faith in his own judgement, the richest and most glorious spot of ground on this earth might never have been discovered, and these lines might never have been written. Had George Washington and his compatriots in 1776 not possessed self-confidence, Cornwallis's armies would have conquered, and the United States of America would be ruled today from a little island lying 3,000 miles away in the East.

A Definite Chief Aim is the starting point of all noteworthy achievement, but self-confidence is the unseen force that coaxes, drives or leads one on and on until the object of the aim is a reality. Without self-confidence, no achievements would ever get beyond the 'aim' stage, and mere aims, within themselves, are worth nothing. Many people have vague sorts of aims, but they get nowhere because they lack the self-confidence to create definite plans for attaining these aims.

Fear is the main enemy of self-confidence. Every person comes into this world cursed, to some extent, with Six Basic Fears, all of which must be mastered before one may develop sufficient self-confidence to attain outstanding success. These Six Basic Fears are:

1. The Fear of Criticism
2. The Fear of Ill Health
3. The Fear of Poverty
4. The Fear of Old Age
5. The Fear of Loss of Love of Someone (ordinarily called jealousy)
6. The Fear of Death

Space will not permit a lengthy description of where these Six Fears came from. In the main, however, they were acquired through the early childhood environment, by teaching, the telling of ghost stories, discussion of 'hellfire' and in many other ways. Fear of Criticism is placed at the head of the list because it is, perhaps, the most common and one of the most destructive of the entire Six Fears. It's said that fear of public speaking is the most common one of all, and clearly Fear of Criticism is at the heart of it. No matter how urgent one's message, or how much a job or a sale depends on it, the same damp palms and halting speech afflict board chairperson and schoolchild. (One classic remedy seems to defuse this paralysing fear, at least temporarily. That is the suggestion that the speaker visualise the audience naked.) It remains a fact that this fear is a self-centred one, and is brought on by pure vanity.

Knowledge of this basic Fear of Criticism brings vast fortunes to the manufacturers of clothing each year, and costs timid people the same amount, because most people lack the personality or the courage to wear clothes that are one season out of style. To some extent this basic Fear of Criticism is employed by the manufacturers of cars who design new models every season, so as to satisfy the status-seekers and those who depend on outward shows of success.

Before you can develop sufficient self-confidence to master the obstacles standing between you and success, you must take an inventory of yourself and find out how many of these Six Basic Fears are standing in your way. A few days of study, thought and reflection will readily enable you to lay your fingers on the particular fear or fears that stand between you and self-confidence. Once you discover these enemies, you may easily eliminate them, through a procedure that will be described later on.

The Fears of Ill Health, Poverty, Old Age and Death are thought by some to be the results of teachings of a bygone age. Though such beliefs persist in certain quarters today, it was even more common in the past for people to be taught that death might bring with it a world consisting of fire and eternal torment. The possibility exists that the effect of this teaching so shocked the sensibilities of the human mind that fear became imbedded in the subconscious and, in that manner, was transmitted from parent to child and thus kept alive from generation to generation. Scientists differ as to the extent that such fears can be transmitted from parent to child, through physical heredity. They are all in accord on this point, however: that the discussion of such matters in the presence of a child is sufficient to plant the fear impulse in its subconscious mind, where nothing but strong resolution and great faith in a belief opposite to the thing feared can eliminate the damage done.

The Fear of Loss of Love of Someone (jealousy) is a holdover from the days of human savagery, when it was man's habit to steal his fellow man's mate by force. The practice of stealing another's mate still exists, to some extent, but the stealing is now done through allurements of one sort or another: a sympathetic ear, too much intimacy at the office, a thoughtful gift, a fine dinner. The spouse may no longer be dragged into a cave by a suitor wielding a club, but those in relationships often intuitively sense the same danger that was present in prehistory. Thus the Fear of Loss of Love (or jealousy) has a biological as well as an economic basis for its existence. Jealousy is a form of insanity, because it is often indulged in without the slightest reason for its existence, linking it often with paranoia. Despite this fact, this fear causes untold suffering, annoyance and failure in this world. To understand the nature of this fear and how one comes by it is a step in the direction of its mastery.

Every student of this philosophy should do a certain amount of collateral reading, selecting biographies of those who have attained outstanding success, because this is sure to disclose the fact that these leaders met with practically every conceivable sort of temporary defeat. Yet, despite these discouraging experiences, they developed self-confidence sufficient to enable them to master every obstacle that stood in their way. Among the recommended classic books of this type are *Compensation*, by Ralph Waldo Emerson, and *The Age of Reason*, by Thomas Paine. These two historic books, alone, help to place the concept of self-confidence within reach. They make it easier to understand why there are but few impossibilities in life, if there are any at all.

CHAPTER 4

THE HABIT OF SAVING

It is an embarrassing admission, but it is true that a poverty-stricken person hasn't got a chance to be considered a noteworthy success – unless that poverty is planned and purposeful. In that case, it's voluntary simplicity, and that's the subject of another book. It may be, and perhaps is, true that money is not success, but unless you have it or can command its use in the ordinary world, you will not get far, no matter what may be your Definite Chief Aim. As business is conducted today – and as civilisation in general stands today – money is an absolute essential for success, and there is no known formula for financial independence except that which is connected, in one way or another, with systematic saving.

The amount saved from week to week or from month to month is not of great consequence, so long as the saving is regular and systematic. This is true because the habit of saving adds something to the other qualities essential for success, which can be had in no other way. It is doubtful if any person can develop self-confidence to the highest possible point without the protection and independence that belongs to those who have saved and are saving money. There is something about the knowledge that one has some money in the bank that gives faith and self-reliance such as can be had in no other way.

The one without money can more easily be exploited and preyed upon. Such a person is at the mercy of everyone who wishes to exploit or prey upon them. If the one who does not save and therefore has no money offers a personal service, there is no alternative to accepting what the purchaser offers. If opportunity to profit by trade or otherwise comes along, it is of no avail to the one who has neither money nor credit, and it must be kept in mind that credit is generally based upon the money one has or its equivalent.

When the Law of Success philosophy was first created, the habit of saving was not included as one of the 17 laws, with the result that thousands of people who experimented with this philosophy found that it carried them almost within reach of their goal of success, only to dash their hopes to pieces on the rocks. For years the author of the course and the creator of the philosophy searched for the reason why the philosophy fell just barely short of its intended purpose. Through many years of experimentation and research, it was finally discovered that one law was lacking, and that was the law of the habit of saving.

When this law was added, the students of the Law of Success philosophy began to prosper without exception, and now untold millions have used the philosophy for the attainment of success, and not one single case of failure has been reported.

The amount of your income is of but little importance if you do not systematically save a portion of it. Ten million a year income is no better than 10 thousand unless a part of it is saved. As a matter of fact, the income of 10 million may be far more disabling for the one who receives it than the very small income, if the entire amount is spent and dissipated, because the manner in which it is spent may very well undermine the health and in other ways destroy the chances of success.

Millions of people have read stories about Henry Ford's stupendous achievements and great wealth, but it is safe to say that not one out of every thousand of these people has taken the trouble or done enough thinking to determine the real basis of Ford's success. Through a test made by the author of the Law of Success philosophy, 500 people were given an outline of the 12 fundamentals that have been largely responsible for Ford's success. In this outline it was pointed out that the amount of cash received each year from the floor sweepings and rubbish taken from the Ford plants amounted to nearly $600,000. Not one of the entire 500 placed any significance upon this fact. Not one of the 500 discovered, or if they did they failed to mention it, the fact that Ford was always a systematic saver of resources.

We know a great deal about people's spending habits but little of the more important habit of saving. Woolworth built one of the highest skyscrapers in the world during his era, and accumulated a fortune of over $100 million dollars by saving the dimes millions of Americans threw away in the rubbish. The habit of spending money is a mania with most people, and this habit keeps their noses to the grindstone all the days of their lives.

Tests have been made that show, conclusively, that the majority of businesspeople will not place their resources or even positions involving responsibilities in other directions in the hands of those who have not formed the habit of saving money. The savings habit is the finest sort of recommendation of anyone of any position. The late James J. Hill (who was well prepared to speak with authority on the subject) said that there is a rule by which anyone may determine whether or not he or she would succeed in life. He said the rule came in the form of a required habit: that of systematically saving money.

CHAPTER 5

INITIATIVE AND LEADERSHIP

All people may be placed in one or the other of two general classes. One is known as 'leaders' and the other as 'followers'. Not often do the followers achieve noteworthy success, and never succeed until they break away from the ranks of the followers and become leaders.

There is a mistaken notion being broadcast in the world among a certain class of people to the effect that people are paid for what they know. This is only partly true, and, like all other half-truths, it does more damage than an out-and-out falsehood. The truth is that people are paid not only for what they know, but more particularly for what they do with what they know, or what they get others to do. Without initiative, no one will achieve success, no matter what he or she may consider success, because he or she will do nothing out of the ordinary, only the mediocre work required in order to have a place to sleep, something to eat and clothes to wear. These three necessities may be had without the aid of initiative and leadership, but the moment people make up their minds to acquire more than the bare necessities of life, they must either cultivate the habits of initiative and leadership or else find themselves hedged in behind a stone wall.

The first step essential in the development of initiative and leadership is that of forming the habit of prompt and firm decision. All successful people have a certain amount of decision-making power. Those who waver between two or more half-baked and more or less vague notions of what they want to do generally end by doing nothing.

There had been 'talk' about building the Panama Canal for many generations, but the actual work of building the canal never got much beyond the talk stage until the late Theodore Roosevelt became President of the United States. With the firmness of decision that was the very warp and woof of his achievements and the real basis of his reputation as a leader, Roosevelt took the initiative. He had a bill framed for Congress to pass, providing the money. He went to work with a spirit of self-confidence, plus a Definite Chief Aim and a definite plan for its attainment, and lo! The much-talked-of Panama Canal became a splendid reality.

It is not enough to have a Definite Chief Aim and a definite plan for its achievement, even though the plan may be perfectly practical and you may have all the necessary ability to carry it through successfully. You must have more than these. You must actually take the initiative and put the wheels of your plan into motion and keep them turning until your goal has been reached.

Study those whom you know to be failures (you'll find them all around you) and observe that, without a single exception, they lack the firmness of decision, even in matters of the smallest importance. Such people usually 'talk' a great deal, but they are very short on performance. 'Deeds, not words' should be the motto of those who intend to succeed in life, no matter what may be their calling, or what has been selected as a Definite Chief Aim.

Lack of decision has often resulted in insanity. Nothing is very bad or dreadful, once one has reached a decision to face the consequences. This truth was demonstrated quite effectively by a man who was condemned to die on death row. When asked how it felt to know that he was to die in another half hour, he replied, 'Well, it does not bother me in the least. I made up my mind that I had to go sometime, and it might as well be now as a few years later, because my life has been nothing but a sad failure and a constant source of trouble anyway. Just think: it will soon all be over.' The man was actually relieved to know that the responsibilities of life to which he had been subjected, and which had brought him to such an ignoble ending, were about to cease.

Prominent and successful leaders are always people who reach decisions quickly, yet it is not to be assumed that quick decisions are always advisable. There are circumstances calling for deliberation, the study of facts connected with the intended decision, and so on. However, after all available facts have been gathered and organised, there is no excuse for delaying decision, and the person who practises the habit of such delay cannot become an effective leader until that shortcoming is mastered.

Julius Caesar had long wanted to conquer the armies of another country, but he faltered because he was not sure of the loyalty of his own armies. Finally he decided upon a plan that would ensure this loyalty. Loading his soldiers on to boats, he set sail for the shores of his enemy, unloaded the soldiers and implements of war, and then gave the order for all the boats to be burned. Turning to his generals, he said, 'Now it is win or perish! We have no choice! Pass the word to your men and let them know that it is the lives of our enemies or our own.' They went into battle and won. Julius Caesar won because he saw to it that all his soldiers had reached a decision to win!

Grant said, 'We will fight it out along these lines if it takes all summer,' and despite his deficiencies he stood by that decision and won!

When asked by one of his sailors what he would do if they saw no signs of land by the following day,

Columbus replied, 'If we see no land tomorrow we will sail on and on.' He, too, had a Definite Chief Aim, a definite plan for its attainment, and he had reached a decision not to turn back.

It is a known fact that many cannot do their best until they are actually fighting with their backs to the wall, under the stress of the most urgent necessity. Impending danger will enable ordinary humans to develop super-human courage and strength of both body and mind far out of proportion to that normally used.

Napoleon, caught by surprise when he discovered that there was a deep camouflaged ditch just ahead of the line of march of his armies, gave the order for his cavalry to charge. He waited until the dead bodies of men and horses filled the ditch, then marched his soldiers across and whipped the enemy. That required a serious decision; moreover, it required instantaneous decision. One minute of faltering or hesitation and he would have been flanked by the enemy and captured. He did the unexpected, the 'impossible', and got away with it.

In the field of selling nearly all salespeople are met with the stereotyped alibi: 'I will think it over and let you know later,' which really means that 'I do not wish to buy, but I lack the courage to reach a definite decision and frankly say so.' Being a leader, and understanding the value of initiative, the real sales leader does not take such alibis for an answer. That salesperson begins, immediately, to assist the prospective purchaser in the process of 'thinking it over' and in short order the job is completed and the sale has been made.

CHAPTER 6

IMAGINATION

No one ever accomplished anything, created anything, built any plan or developed a Definite Chief Aim without the use of imagination! Everything ever created or built was first mentally envisioned – through imagination!

Years before his business became a reality, the late John Wanamaker saw in his imagination, in practically all of its details, the gigantic business that for so many years bore his name. Despite the fact that he was then without the capital to create such a business, he managed to get it and lived to see the business he had dreamed of in his mind become a splendid reality.

In the workshop of the imagination one may take old, well-known ideas or concepts, or parts of ideas, and combine them with still other old ideas or parts of ideas, and out of this combination create that which seems to be new. This process is the major principle of all invention.

One may have a Definite Chief Aim and a plan for achieving it, may possess self-confidence in abundance, may have a highly developed habit of saving, and qualities of both initiative and leadership. However, if the element of imagination is missing, these other qualities will be held useless because there will be no driving force to shape their use. In the workshop of the imagination, all plans are created, and without such plans no achievement is possible except by mere accident.

Witness the manner in which the imagination can be used as both the beginning and the end of successful plans: Clarence Saunders, who created the chain of Piggly-Wiggly supermarkets, conceived the idea on which the stores were based, or rather borrowed it, from the cafeteria restaurant system. What happened was that, while working as a grocer's helper, Mr Saunders went into a cafeteria for lunch. Standing in line, waiting for his turn at the food counters, the wheels of his imagination began to turn, and he reasoned to himself something like this:

People seem to like to stand in line and help themselves. Moreover, I see that more people can be served this way, with fewer salespeople. Why would it not be a good idea to introduce this plan in the grocery business, so people could come in, wander around with a basket, pick up what they wanted, and pay on the way out?

Then and there, with that bit of elementary 'imagining', Mr Saunders sowed the seed of an idea which later became the Piggly-Wiggly stores system and made him a multimillionaire in the bargain.

'Ideas' are the most profitable products of the human mind, and they are all created in the imagination. The chain of stores created by F. W. Woolworth was the result of imagination. Woolworth was working as a salesman in a retail store. The owner of the store complained that he had a considerable amount of old, unsaleable merchandise on hand that was in the way, and was about to throw some of it into the bin to be consigned to the furnace, when Woolworth's imagination began to function.

'I have an idea,' said he, 'how to make this merchandise sell. Let's put it all on a table and place a big sign on the table saying that all articles will be sold at 10 cents each.'

The idea seemed feasible, so it was tried. It worked satisfactorily, and then further development began. This resulted, finally, in the big chain of Woolworth stores that eventually appeared throughout the entire country and made the man who used his imagination a classic success story and a household name. Ideas are valuable in any business. People who strike out to cultivate the power of imagination, out of which ideas are born, will sooner or later find themselves headed towards financial success backed with tremendous power.

Thomas A. Edison invented the incandescent electric light bulb by the use of his imagination, when he assembled two old and well-known principles in a combination in which they had never before been associated. A brief description of just how this was accomplished will help you to envision the manner in which the imagination may be made to solve problems, overcome obstacles and lay the foundation for great achievements in any undertaking.

The basic idea behind the light bulb was not new. Edison discovered, as other experimenters had before him, that a light could be created by applying electrical energy to a wire, thus heating the wire to a white heat. The trouble, however, came because of the fact that no one had found a way to control the heat. The wire soon burned out when heated sufficiently to give a clear light.

After many years of experimentation, Edison happened to think of the well-known old method of burning charcoal. He saw, instantly, that this principle held the secret to the control of heat that was needed to create a light by applying electrical power to a wire. Charcoal is made by placing a pile of wood on the ground, setting the wood on fire, and then covering it over with dirt, thereby cutting off most of the oxygen from the fire. The wood burns slowly, but it cannot blaze and the stick cannot burn up entirely because there can be no combustion where there is no oxygen, and but little combustion where there is but little oxygen.

With this knowledge in mind, Edison went into his laboratory and placed the wire that he'd been experimenting with inside a vacuum tube, thus cutting off all the oxygen. He then applied the electrical power, and lo! He had a perfect incandescent light bulb. The wire inside the bulb could not burn up because there was no oxygen inside to create combustion sufficient to burn it up. Thus it happened that one of the most useful of modern inventions was created by combining two principles in a new way.

There is nothing absolutely new! Whatever seems to be new is but a combination of ideas or elements of something old. This is literally true in the creation of business plans, invention, the manufacture of metals and everything else created by humankind.

What is known as a 'basic' patent, meaning a patent that embraces really new and previously undiscovered principles, is rarely offered for record at the Patent Office. Most of the hundreds of thousands of patents applied for and granted every year involve nothing more than a new arrangement or combination of old and well-known principles that have been used many times before in other ways and for other purposes. When Mr Saunders created his Piggly-Wiggly stores system, he did not even combine two ideas; he merely took an old idea that he saw in use and gave it a new setting, or in other words, put it to a new use, but this required imagination.

To cultivate the imagination so it will eventually suggest ideas on its own initiative, you should make it your business to keep a record of all the useful, ingenious and practical ideas you see in use in other lines of work outside of your own occupation, as well as in connection with your own work. Start with an ordinary, pocket-size notebook, and catalogue every idea, concept or thought that occurs to you that is capable of practical use, and then take these ideas and work them into new plans. By and by the time will come when the powers of your own imagination will go into the storehouse of your subconscious mind, where all the knowledge you have ever gathered is stored. Your imagination will assemble this knowledge into new combinations, and hand over to you the results in the shape of brand new ideas, or what appear to be new ideas.

This procedure is practical because it has been followed successfully by some of the best-known leaders, inventors and business leaders. 'Everything you can imagine is real,' said Picasso.

Let us here define the word imagination as 'the workshop of the mind wherein may be assembled, in new and varying combinations, all ideas, thoughts, plans, facts, principles and theories known to humankind'. A single combination of ideas, which may be merely parts of old and well-known ideas, may be worth anything from a few cents to a few millions of dollars. Imagination is the one faculty on which there is no set price or value. It is the most important of the faculties of the mind, for it is here that all of our motives are given the impulse necessary to turn them into action.

The dreamer who does nothing more than dream uses imagination, yes. But the dreamer falls short of utilising this great faculty efficiently because the impulse to put thoughts into action is missing. Here is where initiative enters and goes to work, providing he or she is familiar with the Laws of Success and understands that ideas, of themselves, are worthless until put into action.

The dreamer who creates practical ideas must back up these ideas with three of the laws that have preceded this one, namely:

1. The Law of the Importance of a Definite Chief Aim
2. The Law of Self-confidence
3. The Law of Taking Initiative and Leadership

Without the influence of these three laws, no one may put thoughts and ideas into action, even though the power to dream, imagine and create may be highly developed.

It is your business to succeed in life! How? That is something you must answer for yourself, but, in the main, you must proceed somewhat along these lines:

1. Adopt a definite purpose and create a definite plan for its attainment.
2. Take the initiative and begin putting your plan into action.
3. Back your initiative with belief in yourself and in your ability to successfully complete your plan.

No matter who you are, what you are doing, how much your income is or how little money you have, if you have a sound mind and if you are capable of using your imagination, you can gradually make a place for yourself that will command respect and give you all the worldly goods that you need. There is no trick connected with this. The procedure is simple, as you may start with a very simple, elementary idea, plan or purpose, and gradually develop it into something more impressive.

What if your imagination is not sufficiently developed, at this time, to enable you to create some useful invention? You can begin exercising this faculty anyway, by using it to create ways and means of improving the methods of performing your present work, whatever it may be. Your imagination will grow strong in proportion to the extent that you command it and direct it into use. Look about you and you will find plenty of opportunities to exercise your imagination. Do not wait for someone to show you what to do, but use vision and let your imagination suggest what to do. Do not wait for someone to pay you for using your imagination! Your real pay will come from the fact that every time you use it constructively in creating new combinations of ideas, it will grow stronger. If you keep up this practice, the time will soon come when your services will be sought eagerly, at any price within reason.

If a barber or hair stylist works in a unisex salon, for example, it may seem to him or her that there is little opportunity to use imagination. Nothing could be further from the truth. As a matter of fact, anyone holding such a position may give his or her imagination the finest sort of exercise by making a point of cultivating every customer who enters the salon in such a manner that the customer will repeatedly return. Moreover, the stylist may go a step further and work out ways and means of bringing in one new customer each day, or even one a week, or one a month, and in that manner very materially and quickly add to the salon's income. Sooner or later, through this sort of exercise of imagination – backed up by self-confidence and initiative, plus a Definite Chief Aim – the one who follows this practice will be sure to create some new plan that will draw new hair salon customers from far and near, and will then be on the great road to success.

A complete analysis of occupations shows that the most profitable occupation on earth, taken as a whole, is that of sales. The one whose fertile mind and imagination create a new and useful invention may not have sufficient ability to market that invention, and may therefore have to dispose of it for a mere pittance, as is, in fact, so often the case. But the one who has the ability to market that invention may (and generally does) make a fortune out of it. Anyone who can create plans and ideas that will cause the number of patrons of any business to constantly increase, and who is able to send all the patrons away satisfied, is well on the way to success, regardless of the commodity, service or wares that are sold there.

It is not the purpose of this brief outline of the Law of Success philosophy to show the student what to do and how to do it, but to list the general rules of procedure applied in all successful undertakings so anyone may understand them. These rules are simple and easily adopted by anyone.

CHAPTER 7

ENTHUSIASM

The true meaning of 'enthusiasm' gives this quality an importance that far surpasses the cheerleading attitude this word too often brings to mind. Rooted in the Greek, it means 'inspired', and contains no less than the word for the Creator. Those who come by it naturally are fortunate indeed.

It seems more than a mere coincidence that the most successful people in all walks of life – and particularly in the area of sales – are of the enthusiastic type. Enthusiasm is a driving force that not only gives greater power to the one who has it, but is also contagious and affects all whom it reaches. Enthusiasm for the work in which one is engaged takes the drudgery out of that work. It has been observed that even labourers engaged in the toilsome job of ditch digging can take the drabness out of their work by singing as they work.

When the Yanks went into action during World War I, they went in singing and full of enthusiasm. This was too much for the war-worn soldiers who had been in the field long enough for their enthusiasm to wear off, and they made poor match indeed for the Yanks.

At the turn of the 20th century, the Filene Department Store in Boston was opened with music furnished by the store band every morning during the summer months. The salespeople danced to the music and, when the doors were finally opened for business, the patrons of the store met a jolly crowd of enthusiastic, smiling salespeople, many of whom still hummed the tune to which they had been dancing a few minutes before. This spirit of enthusiasm remained with the salespeople throughout the day, lightening their work and thereby cheering their customers. These days the muzak piped into stores is carefully chosen to have the same effect.

During the same period, it was found that by introducing music with the aid of bands, orchestras and so on into the plants where war materials were being made, production was stimulated, in some instances as much as 50 per cent above normal. Moreover, it was discovered that the workers not only turned out much more work during the day, but also that they came to the end of the day without fatigue, many of them whistling or singing on their way home. Enthusiasm gives greater power to one's efforts, no matter what sort of work one may be engaged in.

Enthusiasm is simply a high rate of mental vibration. The starting point of enthusiasm is 'motive', or well-defined desire. On pages 67–8 may be found a complete list of the mind stimulants that will induce the state of mind known as enthusiasm, the greatest of which is sexual desire. People who do not feel a strong desire for sexual contact are seldom, if ever, capable of becoming highly enthusiastic over anything. Transmutation of the great driving force of sex desire is the basis of practically all the works of genius. (By 'transmutation' is meant the switching of thought from sexual contact to any other form of physical action.)

The importance of enthusiasm, as one of the 17 essentials of the Law of Success, is explained in the chapter on the Master Mind. The strange phenomenon felt by those who coordinate their efforts in a spirit of harmony, for the purpose of availing themselves of the Master Mind principle, is felt as the high rate of mental vibration known as enthusiasm.

It is a well-known fact that people succeed most readily when engaged in an occupation they enjoy, and this for the reason that they readily become enthusiastic over that which they like best. Enthusiasm is also the basis of creative imagination. When the mind is vibrating at a high rate, it is receptive to similar high rates of vibration from outside sources, thus providing a favourable condition for creative imagination. It will be observed that enthusiasm plays an important part in four of the other principles constituting the Law of Success philosophy, namely, the Master Mind, imagination, accurate thought and pleasing personality.

Enthusiasm, to be of value, must be controlled and

directed to definite ends. Uncontrolled enthusiasm may be, and generally is, destructive. The acts of so-called 'bad boys' are nothing more or less than uncontrolled enthusiasm. The wasted energy of this uncontrolled enthusiasm expressed by the majority of young men through promiscuous sexual contact – and sexual desire not expressed through contact – is sufficient to lift them to high achievement, if only this urge were harnessed and transformed.

The next chapter, on self-control, appropriately follows the subject of enthusiasm, as much self-control is necessary in the mastery of enthusiasm.

CHAPTER 8

SELF-CONTROL

Lack of self-control has brought grief to more people than any other shortcoming known to the human race. This evil shows itself, at one time or another, in every person's life.

Every successful person must have some sort of a balance wheel for their emotions. When a person 'loses their temper', something takes place in the brain which should be better understood. When a person becomes extremely angry, certain glands triggered by negative emotions begin to empty their contents into the blood, and if this is kept up for any great length of time, the amount will be sufficient to do serious damage to the entire system, sometimes resulting in death.

The blood coagulates at a time like this, which accounts for one turning white and red in the face, alternately, as the flow of blood throughout the body is temporarily checked. No doubt Nature created this system for the protection of the young human race during the savage stage of development, when anger usually preceded a terrific fight with some other savage, which might mean opening of the veins and loss of blood. Scientists have found, by experiment, that a dog will, when tormented until it becomes angry, throw off enough poison with each exhalation of breath to kill a guinea pig.

But there are other reasons why one should develop self-control. For example, the one who lacks self-control may be easily mastered by one who has such control, and tricked into saying or doing that which may later be embarrassing. Success in life is very largely a matter of harmonious negotiation with other people, and this requires self-control in abundance.

The author of the Law of Success philosophy once observed a long line of angry women in front of the 'complaint desk' of a large department store. Watching at a distance, it was seen that the young woman who was hearing the complaints kept sweetly cool and smiled all the while, notwithstanding the fact that some of the women were very abusive. One by one this young woman directed the women to the right department, and she did it with such poise that it caused the author to walk up closer where he could see just what was happening. Standing just behind the young woman at the complaint desk was another young woman who was also listening to the conversations, and making notes and passing them over the shoulder of the young woman who was actually handling the desk.

These notes contained the gist of each complaint,

minus the vitriol and abuse of the person making the complaint. It turned out the woman at the desk was stone deaf! She was getting all the facts that she needed through her assistant, at her back. The manager of the store said that this was the only system he had found that enabled him to handle the complaint desk properly, as human nerves were not strong enough to listen all day long, day in and day out, to abusive language without causing the person doing the listening to become angry, lose self-control and 'strike back'.

An angry person is suffering from a degree of temporary insanity, and therefore hardly capable of diplomatic negotiation with others. For this reason the one who has no self-control is an easy victim of the one who has such control. No one may become powerful without first gaining control of the self.

Self-control is also a 'balance wheel' for the person who is too optimistic and whose enthusiasm needs checking, for it is possible to become entirely too enthusiastic; so much so that one becomes a bore to all those nearby.

CHAPTER 9

THE HABIT OF DOING MORE THAN PAID FOR

This law is a stumbling block on which many a promising career has been shattered. There is a general inclination among people to perform as little service as they can get away with. But, study these people carefully and you will observe that, while they may actually 'get by' temporarily, they do not get anything else.

There are two major reasons why all successful people must practise this law, as follows:

1. Just as an arm or a limb of the body grows strong in exact proportion to its use, so does the mind grow strong through use. By rendering the greatest possible amount of service, the faculties through which the service is rendered are put into use and, eventually, become strong and accurate.

2. By rendering more service than that for which you are paid, you will be turning the spotlight of favourable attention upon yourself, and it will not be long before you will be sought with impressive offers for your services, and there will be a continuous market for those services.

'Do the thing and you shall have the power,' was the admonition of Emerson, to this day our greatest philosopher. That is literally true! Practice makes perfect. The better you do your work, the more adept you become at doing it, and this, in time, will lead to such perfection that you will have but few, if any, equals in your field of endeavour. By rendering more service and better service than that for which you are paid, you thereby take advantage of the Law of Increasing Returns through the operation of which you will eventually be paid, in one way or another, for far more service than you actually perform.

This is no mere inventive theory. It actually works out in the most practical tests. You must not imagine, however, that the law always works instantaneously. You may render more service and better service than you are supposed to render for a few days, then discontinue the practice and go back to the old, usual habit of doing as little as can be safely trusted to get you by, and the results will in no way benefit you. But if you adopt the habit as a part of your life's philosophy, and let it become known by all who know you that you render such service out of choice – not as a matter of accident, but by deliberate intent – you will soon see keen competition for your service.

You'll observe that it's not easy to find very many people rendering such service, which is all the better for you, because you will stand out in bold contrast with practically all others who are engaged in work similar to yours. Contrast is a powerful law, and you may, in this manner, profit by contrast.

Some people set up the weak but popular argument that it does not pay to render more service and better service than one is paid for because it is not appreciated. They add that they work for people who are selfish and will not recognise such service. Splendid! The more selfish an employer is, the more inclined he or she will be to continue to employ a person who makes a point of rendering such service, unusual both in quantity and quality. This very selfishness will impel such an employer to recognise such services. However, if the employer should happen to be the proverbial exception, one who has not sufficient vision to analyse employees, then it is only a matter of time until all who render such service will attract the attention of other employers who will gladly reward them.

Careful study of the lives of successful men has shown that faithfully practising this one law alone has brought the compensations with which success is usually measured. If the author of this philosophy had to choose one of the 17 Laws of Success as being the most important, and had to discard all the others except the one chosen, he would, without a moment's hesitation, choose this Law of Rendering More Service and Better Service than Paid For.

CHAPTER 10

THE PERSONALITY OF SUCCESS

A pleasing personality, the personality of success, is a personality that does not antagonise. Personality cannot be defined in one word, or with half a dozen words, for it represents the sum total of all one's characteristics, good and bad. Your personality is totally unlike any other personality. It is the sum total of qualities, emotions, characteristics, appearances, and so on, that distinguish you from all other people on earth.

Your clothes form an important part of your personality: the way you wear them, the harmony of colours you select, the quality and many other details all go to indicate much that is intrinsically a part of your personality. Psychologists claim that they can accurately analyse any person, in many important respects, by turning that person loose in a clothing store that sells a great variety and where the subject has instructions to select the clothes freely.

Your facial expression, as shown by the lines of your face, or the lack of lines, forms an important part of your personality. Your voice – its pitch, tone, volume – and the language you use form important parts of your personality, because they mark you instantly, once you have spoken, as a person of refinement or the opposite.

The manner in which you shake hands constitutes an important part of your personality. If, when shaking hands, the hand you offer is limp and lifeless as a dead fish, you are displaying a personality that shows no sign of enthusiasm or initiative.

A pleasing personality usually may be found in the person who speaks gently and kindly, selecting refined words that do not offend, in a modest tone of voice; who selects clothing of appropriate style and colours that harmonise. One who is unselfish and not only willing, but desirous of serving others; who is a friend of all humanity, the rich and the poor alike, regardless of politics, religion or occupation. Who refrains from speaking unkindly of others, either with or without cause; who manages to converse without being drawn into vulgar conversations or useless arguments on such debatable subjects as religion and politics. Who sees both the good and the bad in people, but makes due allowance for the latter; who seeks neither to reform nor to reprimand others; who smiles frequently and deeply.

Who loves music and little children; who sympathises with all who are in trouble and forgives acts of unkindness; who willingly grants others the right to do as they please as long as no one's rights are interfered with. Who earnestly strives to be constructive in every thought and deed; who encourages others and spurs them on to greater and better achievement in their chosen line of work.

A pleasing personality is something that can be acquired by anyone who has the determination to learn how to negotiate his or her way through life without friction, with the object of getting along peacefully and quietly with others. One of the best-known and most successful men in America once said that he would prefer a pleasing personality, as it is defined in this course, to the college degree that was awarded him more than 50 years ago by Harvard University. It was his opinion that a man could accomplish more with a pleasing personality than he could with a college degree, minus the personality.

The development of a pleasing personality calls for exercise of self-control, because there will be many incidents and many people to try your patience and destroy your good resolutions. The reward is worthy of the effort, however, because one who possesses a pleasing personality stands out so boldly compared to the majority of people that his or her pleasing qualities become all the more pronounced.

When Abraham Lincoln was a young man, he heard that a great lawyer, who was known to be an impressive orator, was to defend a client charged with murder some 40 miles from Lincoln's home. He walked the entire distance to hear this man, who was one of the spellbinders of the South. After he had heard the man's speech, and the orator was on his way out of the court room, Lincoln stepped into the aisle, held out his rough hand, and said, 'I walked forty miles to hear you, and if I were to do it over, I would walk a hundred.' The lawyer looked young Lincoln over, turned up his nose, and, in a supercilious manner, walked out without speaking to Lincoln.

Years later these two met once again, this time in the White House, where this selfsame lawyer had come to petition the President of the United States on behalf of a man who had been condemned to death. Lincoln listened patiently to all the lawyer had to say, and, when he had finished speaking, said, 'I see you have lost none of your eloquence since I first heard you defend a murderer years ago, but you have changed considerably in other ways, because you now seem to be a polite gentleman of refinement, which was not the impression I got of you at our first meeting. I did you an injustice, perhaps, for which I now ask your pardon. Meanwhile, I shall sign a pardon for your client and we will call accounts square.'

The lawyer's face turned white and red as he

stammered a brief apology! By his lack of a pleasing personality, at his first meeting with Lincoln, he was guilty of conduct which would have been costly to him, had the incident happened with one less charitable than the great Lincoln.

It has been said, and perhaps correctly, that 'courtesy' represents the most valuable characteristic known to the human race. Courtesy costs nothing, yet it returns dividends that are stupendous if it is practised as a matter of habit, in a spirit of sincerity. A young friend of the author of this philosophy was employed as a service man in one of the petrol stations belonging to a large corporation. One day a big car drove up to his station and the passenger stepped out while the chauffeur told the attendant what kind of fuel he wanted. While the fuel was being pumped, the wealthy passenger entered into conversation with my young friend.

'Do you like your job?' the man inquired.

'Like it, hell!' replied the young man. 'I like it just as much as a dog loves a tomcat.'

'Well,' said the stranger, 'if you do not like your job, why do you work here?'

'Because I am just waiting for something better to turn up,' was the quick rejoinder.

'How long do you think you will have to wait?' the man inquired.

'I dunno how long, but I hope I soon get out of here, because there is no opportunity here for a bright fellow like myself. Why, I'm a high school graduate and I can hold a better position if I had it.'

'Yes?' said the stranger. 'If I offered you a better position than the one you now have, would you be any better off than you are now?'

'I can't say,' replied the young fellow.

'Well,' replied the stranger, 'allow me to offer the suggestion that better positions usually come to those who are prepared to fill them. But I do not believe you are ready for a better position; at least not while you are in your present frame of mind. Perhaps there is a big opportunity for you right where you stand. Let me recommend . . .' And here he recommended a motivational book of that year. 'It may give you an idea that will be useful to you all through life.'

The stranger got into his car and drove away. He was the president of the corporation that owned the petrol station. The young man was talking to his employer, without knowing it, and every word he uttered spoiled his chances of attracting favourable attention.

Later, this same petrol station was placed in the charge of another young man, and it became one of the most profitable service stations operated by that company. The station is, basically, the same as it was before it was turned over to new management. The convenience store inside is exactly the same. The prices charged are the same, but the personality of the man who meets those who drive up to this station for service is not the same.

Practically all success in life hinges, in the final analysis, on personality. A nasty disposition can spoil the chances of the best educated, and such dispositions do spoil not a few.

Good Showmanship – a Part of Personality

Life may be properly called a great drama in which good showmanship is of the utmost importance. Successful people in all callings are generally good showmen; meaning they practise the habit of catering or playing to the crowd. Let us compare some well-known historical figures from different areas on the subject of their ability as showmen. The following once enjoyed outstanding success in their respective callings, because their genius and invention was heightened by their good showmanship:

Theodore Roosevelt
Henry Ford
Thomas A. Edison
Billy Sunday
William Randolph Hearst
George Bernard Shaw

Following is a list of some well-known men, each famous for great ability, but falling short on the score of good showmanship by comparison with the foregoing list:

Woodrow Wilson
Calvin Coolidge
Herbert Hoover
Abraham Lincoln

The inclusion of Lincoln's name here proves that his other sterling qualities took over and placed him at the top of history's list, despite a natural lack of showmanship.

A good showman is one who understands how to cater to the masses. Success is not a matter of chance or luck. It is the result of careful planning and careful staging and able acting of parts by the players in the game.

What is to be done about this defect by someone who is not blessed with a personality which lends itself to able showmanship? Is such a person to be doomed to failure all their life because of Nature's oversight in not blessing them with such a personality?

Not at all! Here is where the principle of the Master Mind comes to the rescue. Those who do not have pleasing personalities may surround themselves with men and women who supply this deficit. The financier J. P. Morgan had a rather pugnacious attitude towards people that prevented him from being a good showman. However, he associated with himself others who supplied all that he lacked in this respect.

Henry Ford was not blessed by Nature with native ability as a good showman, and his personality was not 100 per cent perfect by a long way. However, knowing how to make use of the Master Mind principle, he bridged this defect by surrounding himself with men who did have such ability.

What are the most essential characteristics of good showmanship? First, the ability to appeal to the imagination of the public, and to keep people interested and curious concerning one's activities. Second, a keen sense of appreciation of the value of psychological appeal through advertising. Third, sufficient alertness of mind to enable one to capture and make use of the prejudices, likes and dislikes of the public at the right psychological moment.

Summary of Factors Constituting a Pleasing Personality

Following is a condensed description of the major factors that serve as the basis of a pleasing personality:

1. The manner of shaking hands
2. Clothing and posture of the body

3. Voice – its tone, volume and quality
4. Tactfulness
5. Sincerity of purpose
6. Choice of words, and their appropriateness
7. Poise
8. Unselfishness
9. Facial expression
10. Dominating thoughts (because they register in the minds of other people)
11. Enthusiasm
12. Honesty (intellectual, moral and economic)
13. Magnetism (high rate of vibration due to well-defined, healthy sexuality)

If you wish to try an interesting and perhaps beneficial experiment, analyse yourself and give yourself a grading on each of these 13 factors of a pleasing personality. An accurate checkup on these 13 points might easily bring to one's notice facts which would enable one to eliminate faults that make success impossible.

It will also be an interesting experiment if you form the habit of analysing those whom you know intimately, measuring them by the 13 points here described. Such a habit will, in time, help you to find in other people the causes of both success and failure.

CHAPTER 11

ACCURATE THINKING

The art of accurate thinking is not difficult to acquire, although certain definite rules must be followed. To think accurately one must follow at least two basic principles, as follows:

1. Accurate thinking calls for the separation of facts from mere information.
2. Facts, when ascertained, must be separated into two classes: important and unimportant, or irrelevant.

The question naturally arises, 'What is an important fact?' and the answer is, 'An important fact is any fact that is essential for the attainment of one's Definite Chief Aim or purpose, or which may be useful or necessary in connection with one's daily occupation. All other facts, while they may be useful and interesting, are comparatively unimportant as far as the individual is concerned.'

No one has the right to have an opinion on any subject, unless they have arrived at that opinion by a process of reasoning based upon all the available facts connected with the subject. Despite this fact, however, nearly everyone has opinions on nearly every subject, whether or not they are familiar with those subjects or have any facts connected with them.

Snap judgements and opinions that are not opinions at all, but mere wild conjectures or guesses, are valueless. There's not an idea in a carload of them. Anyone may become an accurate thinker by making it a point to get the facts – all that are available with reasonable effort – before reaching decisions or creating opinions on any subject.

When you hear someone begin a discourse with such generalities as 'I hear that so and so is the case,' or, 'I see by the papers that so and so did so and so,' you may put that person down as one who is not an accurate thinker, and their opinions, guesses, statements and conjectures should be accepted, if at all, with a very hefty grain of salt. Be careful, also, that you do not indulge in wild, speculative language that is not based upon known facts. It often requires considerable effort to learn the facts on any subject, which is perhaps the main reason why so few people take the time or go to the trouble to gather facts as the basis of their opinions.

You are presumably studying this philosophy for the purpose of learning how you may become more successful. If that is true then you must break away from the common practices of the masses who do not think and take the time to gather facts as the basis of thought. That this requires effort is freely admitted, but it must be kept in mind that success is not something that one may come along and pluck from a tree, where it has grown of its own accord. Success is something that represents perseverance, self-sacrifice, determination and strong character.

Everything has its price, and nothing may be obtained without paying this price; or, if something of value is thus obtained, it cannot be retained for long. The price of accurate thought is the effort required to gather and organise the facts on which to base the thought.

'How many cars pass this petrol station each day?' the manager of a chain of such stations asked a new employee. 'And on what days is traffic the heaviest?'

'I am of the opinion . . .' the young man began.

'Never mind your opinion,' the manager interrupted. 'What I asked you calls for an answer based upon facts. Opinions are worth nothing when the actual facts are obtainable.'

With the aid of a pocket calculator, this young man began to count the cars that passed his station each day. He went a step further and recorded the number that actually stopped and purchased petrol or oil, giving the figures day by day for two weeks, including Sundays.

Nor was this all! He estimated the number of cars that should have stopped at his station, day by day, for two weeks. Going still further, he created a plan that cost only the price of one-page flyers and that actually increased the number of cars that stopped at his station for the following two weeks. This was not a part of his required duties, but the question he had been asked by his manager had got him thinking, and he made up his mind to profit by the incident.

The young man in question is now a half-owner in a chain of petrol stations, and a moderately wealthy man, thanks to his ability to become an accurate thinker.

CHAPTER 12

CONCENTRATION

The jack-of-all-trades seldom accomplishes much at any trade. Life is so complex, and there are so many ways of dissipating energy unprofitably, that the habit of concentrated effort must be formed and adhered to by all who would succeed.

Power is based upon organised effort or energy. Energy cannot be organised without the habit of concentration of all the faculties on one thing at a time. An ordinary magnifying glass may be used to so focus the rays of the sun that they will burn a hole in a board in a few minutes. Those same rays will not even heat the board until they are concentrated on one spot. The human mind is something like the magnifying glass, because it is the medium through which all the faculties of the brain may be brought together and made to function, in coordinated formation, just as the rays of the sun may be focused on one spot with the aid of that glass.

It is worth considering that all the outstandingly successful people in all walks of life concentrate the major portion of their thoughts and efforts upon some definite purpose, objective or chief aim. Witness the impressive list of men whose success was due to their having acquired and practised the habit of concentration:

- Woolworth concentrated upon the single idea of five- and ten-cent stores and became a creative genius in the retail field.
- Henry Ford concentrated all his energies upon the single aim of creating a cheap but practical car, and that idea made him one of the most powerful and richest men in history.
- Marshall Field concentrated his efforts upon building 'The World's Greatest Store' and was rewarded by tens of millions of dollars, an unthinkable amount at that time.
- Van Heusen concentrated years of effort on the production of a soft collar, at a time when men thought they would never be free of the stiff collar, and the idea made him wealthy in a comparatively short time, and with a name forever synonymous with the chosen product of his concentration.
- Wrigley concentrated his efforts upon the production and sale of a humble packet of chewing gum, and was rewarded by millions of dollars and a memorable place in history for his perseverance.

- Edison concentrated his mind upon the production of 'the talking machine', the electric light, the motion picture and scores of other useful inventions, until they all became realities and assured him of a place at the top of the pantheon.

- Bessemer concentrated his thoughts upon a better way to produce steel, and the Bessemer process is evidence that his efforts were history-making.

- George Eastman concentrated his energy upon radically improving the business of photographs, and this one idea made him a multimillionaire.

- Andrew Carnegie, the child of immigrants, envisioned a great steel industry, concentrated his mind upon that purpose and made tens of millions of dollars.

- James J. Hill, while still working as a telegrapher at 40 dollars a month, concentrated his thoughts upon the dream of a great transcontinental railway system, and kept on thinking about it (and acting on his thought as well) until it became a splendid reality and made him one of the wealthy men of his time.

- Cyrus H.K. Curtis concentrated his efforts upon one idea of producing the best and most popular magazine on earth, and the splendid *Saturday Evening Post* was but one of the results. He not only created a great magazine, but his concentration of thought brought him millions as well.

- Orville Wright concentrated upon one goal: mastering the air with a heavier–than–air machine, and accomplished it against all odds.
- Marconi concentrated his mind upon one thought – sending wireless messages – and countless lives were improved.

Truly, whatever one can imagine, one can create, providing the mind concentrates upon it with determination not to stop short of victory. Great and powerful is the human mind when functioning through the aid of concentrated thought.

- Woodrow Wilson determined to become President of the United States 25 years before he actually occupied the President's chair in the White House, but he kept his mind concentrated upon this one purpose and eventually achieved it.
- Ingersoll concentrated on the production of a good, practical watch that could be sold for one dollar. His idea, plus his concentrated efforts, made of him a multimillionaire.
- E.M. Statler concentrated on the building of hotels that rendered home–like service, and made himself one of the leading hoteliers of the world, to say nothing of many millions of dollars in wealth.
- Rockefeller concentrated his efforts upon the refining and distribution of oil, and his efforts

brought him tens of millions of dollars.

- Russell Conwell concentrated a lifetime of effort on the delivery of his famous lecture, Acres of Diamonds, and that one lecture brought in more than six million dollars at a time when people were being paid in pennies, and rendered the people of his time a service the extent of which can never be estimated in mere money.

- Lincoln concentrated his mind upon freedom for humankind, and saw his task through, though the end proved unfortunate to him.

- Gillette concentrated upon producing a safety razor; the idea made him a multimillionaire and linked his name permanently with all such products.

- William Randolph Hearst concentrated on newspapers, and became king of his field and lord of his manor.

- Helen Keller was born deaf, dumb and blind, but through concentration she learned to 'hear' and to speak, inspiring the world.

So the story might go on and on in one continuous chain as evidence that concentrated effort is profitable. Find out what you wish to do – adopt a Definite Chief Aim – then concentrate all your energies in support of this purpose until it has reached a happy climax.

Observe, in analysing the next law, on cooperation,

the close connection between the principles outlined and those associated with the Law of Concentration.

Wherever a group of people ally themselves in an organised, cooperative spirit for the carrying out of some definite purpose, it will be observed that they are employing the Law of Concentration and, unless they do so, their alliance will be without real power. Raindrops, as they fall through the air – each one for itself, helter-skelter – represent a very great form of energy, but this energy cannot be called real power until those raindrops are collected in a river or dam and made to pour their energy over a wheel in organised fashion; or, until they are confined in a boiler and converted into steam.

Everywhere, regardless of the form in which it is found, power is developed through concentrated energy. Whatever you are doing as your daily occupation, then, do it with all of your attention, with all your heart and soul focused on that one definite thing.

CHAPTER 13

COOPERATION

This is distinctly an age of cooperation in which we are living. The outstanding achievements in business, industry, finance, transportation and politics are all based upon the principle of cooperative effort.

Hardly a week goes by without some corporate merger taking place. Aside from hostile takeovers, these mergers are based upon cooperation, because cooperation brings together in a spirit of harmony of purpose different energies – whether human or mechanical – so that they function as one, without friction.

Marshal Foch was one of the heroes of World War I. The turning point came, as historians will remember, when all the Allied Armies were placed under the direction of Foch, thus ensuring perfectly coordinated effort and cooperation such as would not have been possible under many leaders.

To succeed in a big way in any undertaking means that one must have the friendly cooperation of others. The winning football team is the one that is best coached in the art of cooperation. The spirit of perfect teamwork must prevail in business, or the business will not get very far.

You will observe that some of the preceding laws of this course must be practised as a matter of habit before one can get perfect cooperation from others. For example, other people will not cooperate with you unless you have mastered and apply the Law of a Pleasing Personality, the Personality of Success. You will also notice that enthusiasm and self-control and the habit of doing more than paid for must be practised before you can hope to gain full cooperation from others.

These laws overlap one another, and all of them must be merged into the Law of Cooperation, which means that to gain cooperation from others, one must form the habit of practising the laws named. No one is willing to cooperate with a person who has an offensive personality. No one is willing to cooperate with one who is not enthusiastic, or who lacks self-control. Power comes from organised, cooperative effort! A dozen well-trained soldiers, working with perfectly coordinated effort, can master a mob of a thousand people who lack leadership and organisation.

Education, in all of its forms, is nothing but organised knowledge, or, as it might be stated, cooperative facts! Andrew Carnegie had but little schooling, yet he was a well-educated man because he formed the habit of organising his knowledge and shaping it into a Definite

Chief Aim. He also made use of the Law of Cooperation, as a result of which he made himself a multimillionaire; moreover, he made millionaires of scores of other men who were allied with him in his application of the Law of Cooperation that he so well understood.

It was Andrew Carnegie who gave the author of the Law of Success philosophy the idea upon which the entire philosophy was founded. The event is worth describing, as it involves a newly discovered law that is the real basis of all effective cooperation.

The author went to interview Carnegie for the purpose of writing a story about his industrial career. The first question asked was:

'Mr Carnegie, to what do you attribute your great success?'

'You have asked me a big question,' said Carnegie, 'and before I answer I would like you to define the word "success". Just what do you call success?'

Before the author had time to reply, Carnegie anticipated the reply by saying: 'By success I think you mean my money, do you not?'

The author said, 'Yes, that seems to be the term that stands for success.'

'Oh, well,' replied Carnegie, 'if you merely wish to know how I got my money – if that is what you call success – I can easily answer your question. To begin with, let me tell you that we have, here in this steel business: a Master Mind. This Master Mind is not the mind of any one person, but it is the sum total of the ability, knowledge and experience of nearly a score of men whose minds have been perfectly coordinated so they function as one, in a spirit of harmonious co-operation. These are the ones who manage the various departments of this business. Some of them have been associated with me for many years, while others have not been here so long.

'You may be surprised to know,' Carnegie continued, 'that I have had to try and then try over and over again to find those whose personalities were such that they could subordinate their own interests for the benefit of the business. One of the most important places on our staff had been filled by more than a dozen before one was finally found who could do the work required in that position and at the same time cooperate in a spirit of harmony with the other members of our staff. My one big problem has been, and always will continue to be, the difficulty in securing the services of people who will cooperate, because without cooperation the Master Mind of which I speak could not exist.'

In these words, or their equivalent, as I am quoting from memory, the greatest of all the steel magnates the industry has ever known laid bare the real secret of his stupendous achievements. His statement led this author to a line of research, covering a period of over 20 years, which resulted in the discovery that this same Master

Mind principle is also the secret of the success of most of the other successful leaders of this type who are at the heads of our great industries, financial institutions, railways, banks, department stores, and so on.

It is a fact, although the scientific world may not yet endorse it, that whenever two or more minds are allied towards any undertaking in a spirit of harmony and cooperation, there arises an unseen power that gives greater energy to the undertaking. You may test this out, in your own way, by watching the reaction of your own mind when you are in the presence of those with whom you are friendly. Compare your reaction to what happens when you are in the presence of those whom you do not like. Friendly association inspires one with a mysterious energy not otherwise experienced, and this great truth is the very foundation stone of the Law of Cooperation.

An army that is forced to fight because the soldiers are afraid they will be shot down by their own leaders may be a very effective army, but such an army has never been a match for the army that goes into action of its own accord, with soldiers determined to win because they believe their side ought to win. At the beginning of World War I, the Germans were sweeping everything before them. The German soldiers, at that time, went into action singing. They had been thoroughly 'sold' on the idea of 'kultur'. Their leaders had made them think they were bound to win because they ought to win.

However, as the war went along these same soldiers began to see the light. It began to dawn upon them that the killing off of millions was a serious business. Next, the thought began to creep in that, after all, perhaps their Kaiser was not the ordained agent of God, and that they might be fighting an unjust war. From this point on the tide began to turn. They no longer went into battle singing. They no longer 'felt proud to die for "kultur"', and their end was then a short distance away.

So it is in every walk of life, in every human endeavour. Those who can subordinate their own personalities, subdue their own self-interests and coordinate all their efforts – physical and mental – with those of others in support of a common cause they believe in, have already gone nearly the entire distance towards success.

A few years ago the managing director of a well-known estate agency addressed the following letter to the author:

DEAR MR HILL:

Our firm will give you a cheque for $10,000 if you will show us how to secure the confidence of the public in our work as effectively as you do in yours.

Very cordially,

To this letter the following reply was sent:

DEAR MR J–:

I thank you for the compliment, and while I could use your cheque for $10,000, I am perfectly willing to give you, gratis, what information I have on the subject. If I have unusual ability to gain cooperation from other people, it is because of the following reasons:

1. I render more service than I ask people to pay for.
2. I engage in no transaction, intentionally, that does not benefit all whom it affects.
3. I make no statements that I do not believe to be true.
4. I have a sincere desire in my heart to be of useful service to the greatest possible number of people.
5. I like people better than I like money.
6. I am doing my best to live as well as to teach my own philosophy of success.
7. I accept no favours from anyone without giving favours in return.
8. I ask nothing of any person without having a right to that for which I ask.
9. I enter into no arguments with people over trivial matters.

10. I spread the sunshine of optimism and good cheer wherever and whenever I can.

11. I never flatter people for the purpose of gaining their confidence.

12. I sell counsel and advice to other people, at a modest price, but never offer free advice.

13. While teaching others how to achieve success, I have demonstrated that I can make my philosophy work for myself as well, thus 'practising what I preach'.

14. I am so thoroughly sold on the work in which I am engaged that my enthusiasm over it becomes contagious and others are influenced by it.

If there are any other elements entering into what you believe to be my ability to get the confidence of others, I do not know what they are. Incidentally, your letter raised an interesting question, and caused me to analyse myself as I had never done before. For this reason I refuse to accept your cheque, on the grounds that you have caused me to do something which may be worth many times 10,000 dollars.

Very cordially,
NAPOLEON HILL

In these 14 points may be found the elements that form the basis of all confidence-building relationships. Cooperative effort brings power to those who can get and permanently hold the confidence of great numbers of people. This author knows of no method of inducing others to cooperate, except that which is based upon the 14 points here described.

CHAPTER 14

PROFITING BY FAILURE

A wealthy philosopher by the name of Croesus was the official counsellor to his majesty, King Cyrus. He said some very wise things in his capacity as court philosopher, among them this: 'I am reminded, O king, and take this lesson to heart, that there is a wheel on which the affairs of humans revolve, and its mechanism is such that it prevents anyone from being always fortunate.'

It is true. There is a sort of unseen Fate, or wheel, turning in the lives of all of us, and sometimes it brings us good fortune and sometimes ill fortune, despite anything that we as individual human beings can do. However, this wheel obeys the law of averages, thereby insuring us against continuous ill fortune. If ill fortune comes today, there is hope in the thought that its opposite will come in the next turn of the wheel, or the one following the next, and so on.

Failure is one of the most beneficial parts of a human

being's experience. This is because there are many needed lessons that must be learned before one commences to succeed which could be learned from no teacher other than failure. Failure is always a blessing in disguise, providing it teaches us some useful lesson that we could not or would not have learned without it!

Failure is to life what the kiln is to the potter. It tempers us. However, millions of people make the mistake of accepting failure as final, whereas it is – like most other events in life – transitory, and for this reason should not be accepted as final. Successful people must learn to distinguish between failure and temporary defeat. Every person experiences, at one time or another, some form of temporary defeat, and out of such experiences come some of the greatest and most beneficial lessons.

In truth, most of us are so constituted that if we never experienced temporary defeat (or what some ignorantly call failure), we would soon become so egotistical and independent that we would imagine ourselves more important than Deity. There are a few such people in this world, and it is said of them that they refer to Deity, if at all, as 'Me and God', with heavy emphasis on the 'Me'!

Headaches are beneficial, despite the fact that they are very disagreeable, for the reason that they represent Nature's language. In this case she calls loudly for intelligent use of the human body; particularly of the stomach and tributary organs through which most of us create the majority of physical human ills. It is the same regarding temporary defeat or failure. These are Nature's symbols through which she signals to us that we have been heading in the wrong direction. If we are reasonably intelligent we heed these signals, steer a different course and come, finally, to the objective of our Definite Chief Aim.

The author of this philosophy has devoted more than a quarter of a century to research for the purpose of discovering what characteristics were possessed and employed by the successful men and women in the fields of business, industry, politics, statesmanship, religion, finance, transportation, literature, science and so on. This research has involved the reading of more than 1,000 books of a scientific, business and biographical nature, or an average of more than one such book a week.

One of the most startling discoveries made through this enormous amount of research was the fact that all the outstanding successes, regardless of the field of endeavour in which they were engaged, were people who met with reverses, adversity, temporary defeat and, in some instances, actual permanent failure (as far as they, as individuals, were concerned). Not one single successful person was discovered whose success was attained without the experience of what, in many instances, seemed like unbearable obstacles that had to be mastered.

It was discovered also that these people rose to success in exact ratio to the extent that they met squarely and did not budge from defeat. In other words, success is measured, always, by the extent to which any individual meets and squarely deals with the obstacles that arise in the pursuit of their Definite Chief Aim.

Let us recall a few of the great successes of the world who met with temporary defeat, and some of whom were permanent failures, as far as they, as individuals, were concerned.

Columbus started out to find a shorter passage to India, but discovered America instead. He died a prisoner, in chains, a victim of ignorance.

Thomas A. Edison met with defeat after defeat, more than 10,000 unsuccessful efforts in all, before he made a revolving piece of wax record and reproduce the sound of the human voice. He met with similar defeat before he created the modern incandescent electric light bulb.

Alexander Graham Bell met with years of defeat before he perfected the long-distance telephone.

Woolworth's first five- and ten-cent store project was not a success, and he had to master the most trying obstacles before he finally got his true bearings and rode high on the road to success.

Fulton's steamboat was a flop, and people laughed at him so hard that he had to sneak out at night and conduct his experiments privately.

The Wright brothers smashed many aeroplanes and

suffered much defeat before they created a heavier-than-air flying machine that was practical.

Henry Ford almost starved to death, figuratively if not literally, before he successfully completed his first working model of a car. Nor was this the end of his troubles; he spent years perfecting the famous Model T car that made his fame and fortune.

Do not think, for one moment, that these people rode to success on the wings of plenty, without opposition of the most heart-rending nature. We are too apt to look at leaders in the hour of their triumph without taking into consideration the setbacks, defeats and adversities through which they had to pass before success came.

Napoleon met with defeat after defeat before he made himself the great power that he was, and even then he finally met with permanent failure. At many times, it is recorded in his biographies, he contemplated committing suicide, so great were his disappointments.

The Panama Canal was not built without defeat. Time after time many of the deep cuts fell in and the engineers had to go back and do their work all over again. It looked on many occasions, to those on the outside, as if some of the heavy cuts never could be made to stand up. But perseverance, plus a Definite Chief Aim, finally delivered the most marvellous artificial body of water in the world, viewed from the standpoint of usefulness.

There comes to mind what this author believes to be

the finest poem ever written on the subject of failure. It so thoroughly and clearly states the benefits of defeat that it is here reprinted, as follows:

WHEN NATURE WANTS A MAN!
By Angela Morgan
(Copyright, 1926, by Dodd, Mead and Company, Inc.)

When Nature wants to drill a man,
And thrill a man,
And skill a man.
When Nature wants to mould a man
To play the noblest part;
When she yearns with all her heart
To create so great and bold a man
That all the world shall praise
Watch her method, watch her ways!
How she ruthlessly perfects
Whom she royally elects;
How she hammers him and hurts him,
And with mighty blows converts him
Into trial shapes of day which only Nature
understands.
While his tortured heart is crying
and he lifts beseeching hands
How she bends but never breaks,
When his good she undertakes

How she uses whom she chooses
And with every purpose infuses him,
By every art induces him
To try his splendour out
Nature knows what she's about.

When Nature wants to take a man,
And shake a man, and wake a man;
When Nature wants to make a man
To do the Future's will;
When she tries with all her skill
And she yearns with all her soul
To create him large and whole.
With what cunning she prepares him!
How she goads and never spares him,
How she whets him, and she frets him,
And in poverty begets him.
How she often disappoints
Whom she sacredly anoints,
With what wisdom she will hide him,
Never minding what betide him
Though his genius sob with slighting,
and his pride may not forget!
Bids him struggle harder yet.
Makes him lonely So that only
God's high messages shall reach him,
So that she may surely teach him
What the Hierarchy planned.

Though he may not understand
Gives him passions to command.
Now remorselessly she spurs him
With terrific ardour stirs him
When she poignantly prefers him!

When Nature wants to name a man
And fame a man
And tame a man;
When Nature wants to shame a man
To do his heavenly best
When she tries the highest test
That the reckoning may bring
When she wants a god or king!
How she reins him and restrains him
So his body scarce contains him
While she fires him
And inspires him!
Keeps him yearning, ever burning for a tantalising
goal –
Lures and lacerates his soul.
Sets a challenge for his spirit,
Draws it high when he's near it;
Makes a jungle that he clear it;
Makes a desert that he fear it
And subdue it if he can.
So doth Nature make a man.
Then, to test his spirit's wrath

Hurls a mountain in his path,
Puts a bitter choice before him
And relentless stands o'er him.
'Climb, or perish!' so she says
Watch her purpose, watch her ways!

Nature's plan is wondrous kind
Could we understand her mind
Fools are they who call her blind.
When his feet are torn and bleeding,
Yet his spirit mounts unheeding
All his higher powers speeding,
Blazing newer paths and fine;
When the force that is divine
Leaps to challenge every failure
And his ardour still is sweet,
And love and hope are burning
In the presence of defeat.
Lo, the crisis! Lo, the shout
That must call the leader out.
When the people need salvation
Doth he come to lead the nation.
Then doth Nature show her plan
When the world has found – a man!

Do not be afraid of temporary defeat, but make sure
that you learn some lesson from every such defeat. That
which we call 'experience' consists, largely, of what we

learn by mistakes – our own and those made by others – but take care not to ignore the knowledge that may be gained from mistakes.

CHAPTER 15

TOLERANCE

Intolerance has caused more grief than any of the many other forms of ignorance. Practically all wars grow out of intolerance. Misunderstandings between so-called 'capital' and 'labour' are usually the outgrowth of intolerance. It is impossible for anyone to observe the Law of Accurate Thought without having first acquired the habit of tolerance, for the reason that intolerance causes a person to close the Book of Knowledge and write 'Finis, I know it all!' on the cover.

The most damaging form of intolerance grows out of religious and racial differences of opinion. Civilisation, as we know it today, bears the deep wounds of gross intolerance all through the ages, mostly those of a religious nature. Intolerance is the result of ignorance or, stated conversely, the lack of knowledge. Well-informed people are seldom intolerant because they know that no one knows enough to be entitled to judge others.

Through the principle of social heredity, we inherit, from our environment and through our early religious teachings, our ideas of religion. Our teachers themselves may not be always right, and, if we bear this thought in mind, we would not allow such teachings to influence us to believe that we have a corner on truth, and that people whose teachings on this subject have been different from our own are all wrong.

There are many reasons why one should be tolerant, the chief of them being the fact that tolerance permits cool reason to guide one in the direction of facts, and this, in turn, leads to accurate thinking. Those whose minds have been closed by intolerance, no matter of what brand or nature, can never become accurate thinkers, which is sufficient reason to cause us to master intolerance.

It may not be your duty to be tolerant with other people whose ideas, religious views, politics and racial tendencies are different from yours, but it is your privilege! You do not have to ask permission of anyone to be tolerant; this is something that you control, in your own mind; therefore, the responsibility that goes with the choice is also your own.

Intolerance is closely related to the Six Basic Fears described in the Law of Self-confidence, and it may be stated as a positive fact that intolerance is always the result of either fear or ignorance. There are no exceptions to this rule. The moment another person (providing that person is not intolerant) discovers that you are cursed with intolerance, he or she can easily and quickly mark you as being either the victim of fear and superstition or, what is worse, ignorance!

Intolerance closes the doorway to opportunity in a thousand ways, and shuts out the light of intelligence. The moment you open your mind to facts, and take the attitude that the last word is seldom said on any subject, and that there always remains the chance that still more truth may be learned, you begin to cultivate the Law of Tolerance. If you practise this habit for long you will soon become a thinker, with ability to solve the problems that confront you in your struggle to make a place for yourself in your chosen field of endeavour.

CHAPTER 16

USING THE GOLDEN RULE TO WIN COOPERATION

This is, in some ways, the most important of the 17 Laws of Success. Despite the fact that, for more than 5,000 years, the great philosophers all taught the Law of the Golden Rule, the great majority of people today look upon it as a sort of pretty text for preachers to build sermons on. In truth, the Golden Rule philosophy is based upon a powerful law which, when understood and faithfully practised, will enable anyone to get others to cooperate with them.

It is a well-known truth that most people follow the practice of returning good or evil, act for act. If you slander anyone, you will be slandered in return. If you praise anyone, you will be praised. If you favour someone in business, you will be favoured in return. There are exceptions to this rule, to be sure, but by and large the law works out. Like attracts like. This is in accordance with a great natural law, and it works in every particle of matter and in every form of energy in the universe. The successful attract the successful. Failures attract failures. The professional ne'er-do-well will make a beeline for skid row, where they may associate with others of their kind, even though they may have landed in a strange city, after dark.

The Law of the Golden Rule is closely related to the Law of the Habit of Doing More than Paid for. The very act of rendering more service than you are paid to render puts into operation this law, through which 'like attracts like', which is the selfsame law as that which forms the basis of the Golden Rule philosophy. There is no escape from the fact that those who render more service than they're paid to render eventually will be eagerly sought by those who will be willing to pay for more than is actually done. Compound interest on compound interest is Nature's rate, when she goes to pay the indebtedness incurred through application of this law.

This law is so fundamental, so obvious, yet so simple. It is one of the great mysteries of human nature that it is not more generally understood and practised. Behind its use lie possibilities that stagger the imagination of the most visionary person. Through its use may one learn the real secret – all the secret there is – about the art of getting others to do what we wish them to do.

If you want a favour from someone, make it your business to seek out the person from whom you want the favour and, in an appropriate manner, render that person an equivalent of the favour you wish from them. If they do not respond at first, double the dose and render them another favour, and another, and another, and so on, until finally they will, out of shame if nothing more, come back and render you a favour.

You get others to cooperate with you by first cooperating with them! The foregoing sentence is worth reading a hundred times, for it contains the gist of one of the most powerful laws available to those with the intention of attaining great success.

It may sometimes happen that the particular individual to whom you render useful service will never render you a similar service, but keep this important truth in mind: that even though one person fails to respond, someone else will observe the transaction and, out of a sporting desire to see justice done, or perhaps with a more selfish motive in mind, will render you the service to which you are entitled.

'Whatsoever a man soweth, that shall he also reap!' This is more than mere preaching; it is a great practical truth that may be made the foundation of every successful achievement. From winding pathways or straight, every thought you send out, every deed you perform, will gather a flock of other thoughts or deeds according to its own nature, and come back home to you in due time. There is no escape from this truth. It is as eternal as the universe, as sure of operation as the law of gravity. To ignore it is to mark yourself as ignorant, or indifferent, either of which will destroy your chances of success.

The Golden Rule philosophy is the real basis on which children should be governed. It is also the real basis on which 'children grown tall' should be managed. Through force, or by taking advantage of unfair circumstances, one may build a fortune without observing the Golden Rule, and many do this, but such fortunes cannot bring happiness because ill-gotten gain is bound to destroy the peace of mind of all.

Ideas are the most valuable products of the human mind. If you can create usable ideas and put them to work, you can take whatever you wish for your pay. Wealth created or acquired by the Golden Rule philosophy does not bring with it a flock of regrets, nor does it disturb the conscience and destroy the peace of mind. Fortunate are those who make the Golden Rule their business or professional slogan and then live up to the slogan faithfully, both literally and figuratively, observing the spirit of it as well as the letter.

CHAPTER 17

THE HABIT OF HEALTH

We come now to the last of the 17 factors of success. In previous chapters we have learned that success grows out of power; that power is organised knowledge expressed in definite action. No one can remain intensely active very long without good health. The mind will not function properly unless it has a sound body in which to function. Practically all of the other 16 factors which enter into the building of success depend, for their successful application, upon a healthy body.

Good health is dependent, in the main, upon:

1. Proper food and fresh air
2. Regularity of elimination
3. Proper exercise
4. Right thinking

It is not the purpose of this chapter to present a treatise on how to remain healthy, as that is a task belonging to the specialists in physical and mental health. However, no harm can be done by calling attention to the fact that poor health is usually superinduced by poor elimination. People who live in cities and eat processed foods will find it necessary to constantly aid nature in the process of regular elimination, preferably in healthy ways. A great many incidences of headaches, sluggishness, loss of energy and similar feelings are due to autointoxication, or intestinal poisoning through improper elimination.

Most people eat too much. Such people will find it helpful if they go on a 10-day fast about three times a year, during which time they will refrain from taking food of any nature whatsoever. The experience of fasting will bring to all who have never tried it health-building values which can be attained in no other way. No one should experiment with fasting, dieting or any other form of self-administered therapeutics, though, except under the direction of a health care professional.

Sexual Energy – A Health-builder

As a closing thought for this chapter, the author has chosen to inject a very brief statement concerning the therapeutic value of sexual energy. The justification for such a theory is as follows.

It is a well-known fact that thought is the most powerful energy available to humankind. It is equally as well known that negative thoughts of worry and envy and hatred and fear will destroy the digestive processes and bring about illness; this by reason of the fact that negative thought inhibits the flow of certain glandular contents that are essential in the digestive processes.

Negative thoughts cause 'short circuits' in the nerve lines that carry nervous energy (or life force) from the central distributing station, the brain, to all parts of the body, where this energy performs its natural task of nourishment and of removal of worn-out cells and waste matter.

Sexual energy is a highly vitalising, positive force when activated during the period of sexual contact. Because it is powerful, it sweeps over the entire nervous system of the body and unties any 'short circuits' that may exist in any of the nerve lines, thus ensuring a complete flow of nervous energy to all parts of the body.

Sexual emotion is the most powerful of all the human emotions, and when it is actively engaged it reaches and vitalises every cell in every organ of the body, thereby causing the organs to function in a normal manner. Total sexual abstinence was not one of Nature's plans, and those who do not understand this truth usually pay for their ignorance out of a trust fund that Nature provided for the maintenance of health.

Thought controls all voluntary movements of the body. Are we in accord on this statement? Very well, if thought controls all voluntary movements of the body, may it not also be made to control, or at least materially influence, all involuntary movements of the body? Thoughts of a negative nature, such as fear, worry and anxiety, not only inhibit the flow of the digestive juices, but they also 'tie knots' in the nerve lines which carry nervous energy to the various organs of the body. Thoughts of a positive nature untie these knots in the nerve lines and permit the nervous energy to pass through. Sexual feeling is the most powerful form of positive thought. It is Nature's own 'medicine', proof of which is obvious if one will observe the state of mind and the perfectly relaxed condition of the body following sexual contact.

Brief as it is, the foregoing statement should be made the starting point for some intelligent analysis of this subject by the reader of this book. Let us be open-minded on this subject of sex. No one has the last word on the subject; most of us do not even know the first word. Therefore, let us not pass judgement on a subject concerning which we know so very little until we have at least done some intelligent thinking about it. For all we know, both poverty and ill health may be mastered through a complete understanding of the subject of sexual energy, and this for the reason that sex energy is the most powerful mind stimulant known.

THE 30 MOST COMMON CAUSES OF FAILURE

Through the foregoing pages you have had a brief description of the 17 factors through which success is attained. Now let us turn our attention to some of the factors that cause failure. Check the list and you will perhaps find here the cause of any failure, or temporary defeat, that you may have experienced. The list is based upon accurate analysis of over 20,000 failures, and it covers men and women in every calling.

1. Unfavourable hereditary foundation (This cause of failure stands at the head of the list. Bad breeding is a handicap against which there is but little remedy, and it is one for which the individual, unfortunately, is not responsible.)

2. Lack of a well-defined purpose, or definite major aim towards which to strive
3. Lack of the ambition to aim above mediocrity
4. Insufficient education
5. Lack of self-discipline and tact, generally manifesting itself through all sorts of excesses, especially in sexual desires and eating
6. Ill health, usually due to preventable causes
7. Unfavourable environment during childhood, when character was being formed, resulting in vicious habits of body and mind
8. Procrastination
9. Lack of persistence and the courage to take responsibility for one's failures
10. Negative personality
11. Lack of a well-defined sexual urge
12. An uncontrollable desire to get something for nothing, usually manifesting itself in habits of gambling
13. Lack of decision-making ability
14. One or more of the Six Basic Fears described on page 83
15. Poor selection of a mate in marriage
16. Overcaution, destroying initiative and self-confidence
17. Poor selection of associates in business
18. Superstition and prejudice, generally traceable to lack of knowledge of natural laws

19. Wrong selection of occupation
20. Dissipation of energies, through lack of understanding of the Law of Concentration, resulting in what is commonly known as a 'jack of all trades'
21. Lack of thrift
22. Lack of enthusiasm
23. Intolerance
24. Intemperance in eating, drinking and sexual activities
25. Inability to cooperate with others in a spirit of harmony
26. Possession of power that was not acquired through self-effort, as in the case of one who inherits wealth, or is placed in a position of power to which they are not entitled by merit
27. Dishonesty
28. Egotism and vanity
29. Guessing instead of thinking
30. Lack of capital

Some may wonder why 'lack of capital' was placed at the bottom of the list. The answer is that anyone who can qualify with a reasonably high grade on the other 29 causes of failure can always get all the capital needed for any purpose whatsoever.

The above list does not include all the causes of failure, but it does represent the most common causes.

Some may object that 'unfavourable luck' should have been added to the list, but the answer to this complaint is that luck – or the Law of Chance – is subject to mastery by all who understand how to apply the 17 factors of success. However, in fairness to those who may never have had the opportunity to master the 17 factors of success, it must be admitted that luck, or an unfavourable turn of the wheel of chance, is sometimes the cause of failure.

Those who are inclined to attribute all their failures to 'circumstances' or luck should remember the blunt injunction laid down by Napoleon, who said, 'To hell with circumstances, I create circumstances.' Most 'circumstances' and unfavourable results of luck are also self-made. Let us not forget this!

Here is a statement of fact, and a confession, that is well worth remembering. The Law of Success philosophy – which has, to date, rendered useful service to untold millions all over this earth – is very largely the result of nearly 20 years of so-called failure upon the part of the author. In the more extensive course on the Law of Success philosophy, under the lesson on 'Profiting by Failure', the student will observe that the author met with failure and adversity and reverses so often that he might have been justified in crying out, 'Luck is against me!' Seven major failures and more scores of minor failures than the author can, or cares to, remember, laid the foundation for a philosophy which has brought success to so many generations of people, including the author! 'Bad luck' has been harnessed and put to work, and the whole world is now paying substantial monetary tribute to the man who ferreted out the happy thought that even luck can be changed, and failures can be capitalised upon.

'There is a wheel on which the affairs of men revolve, and its mechanism is such that it prevents any man from being always fortunate.' True enough! There is such a wheel of life, but it is rotating continuously. If this wheel brings misfortune today, it can be made to bring good fortune tomorrow. If this were not true, the Law of Success philosophy would be a farce and a fake, offering nothing but false hope.

The author was once told that he would always be a failure because he was born under an unfavourable star! Something must have happened to act as an antidote to the bad influence of that star, and something has happened. That 'something' is the power to master obstacles by first mastering self, which grew out of the understanding and application of the Law of Success philosophy. If the 17 factors of success can offset the bad influence of a star for this author, they can do the same for you, or for any other person.

Blaming our misfortunes on the influence of stars is just another way of acknowledging our ignorance or our laziness. The only place that stars can bring you bad luck is in your own mind. You have possession of that mind, and it has the power to master all the bad influences standing between you and success, including that of the stars.

If you really wish to see the cause of your bad luck and misfortunes, do not look up towards the stars; look in a mirror! You are the master of your fate! You are the captain of your soul. And this by reason of the fact that you have a mind which you, alone, control, and this mind can be stimulated and made to form a direct contact with all the power you need to solve any problem that may confront you. The person who blames his or her troubles upon stars thereby challenges the existence of Infinite Intelligence, or God, if you prefer that name.

The Mystery of the Power of Thought

In front of the author's study, at Broadway and Forty-fourth Street, in New York City, stands the Paramount Building; a great tall, impressive building that serves as a daily reminder of the power of thought. Come, stand with me by the window of my study and let us analyse this modern skyscraper. Tell me, if you can, of what materials the building is constructed. Immediately you will say, 'Why, it is built of brick and steel girders and plate glass and timber,' and you will be partly right, but you have not told the entire story.

The brick and steel and other materials that went into the physical portion of the building were of course necessary, but before any of those materials were laid into place, the building, in its entirety, was constructed of another sort of material. It was first built in the mind of Adolph Zukor, out of the intangible stuff known as thought.

Everything you have or ever will have, good or bad, was attracted to you by the nature of your thoughts. Positive thoughts attract positive, desirable objects; negative thoughts attract poverty and misery and a flock of other sorts of undesirable objects. Your brain is the magnet to which everything you possess clings, and, make no mistake about this, your brain will not attract success while you are thinking of poverty and failure.

All people are exactly where they are as the result of their own dominating thoughts, just as surely as night follows day. Thought is the only thing that you absolutely control, a statement of fact that we repeat because of its great significance. You do not control, entirely, the money you possess, or the love and friendship that you enjoy. You had nothing to do with your coming into the world and you will have but little to do with the time of your going. But you do have everything to do with the state of your own mind. You can make that mind positive or you can permit it to become negative, as the result of outside influences and suggestions. Divine Providence gave you supreme control of your own mind, and with this control you were given the responsibility that is now yours to make the best use of it.

In your own mind you can fashion a great building, similar to the one which stands in front of the author's study, and then transform that mental picture into a reality, just as Adolph Zukor did, because the material out of which he constructed the Paramount Building is available to every human being. Moreover, it is free. All you have to do is appropriate it and put it to your use. This universal material, as we have said, is the power of thought.

The difference between success and failure is largely a matter of the difference between positive and negative thought. A negative mind will not attract a fortune. Like attracts like. Nothing attracts success as quickly as success. Poverty begets more poverty. Become successful and the whole world will lay its treasures at your feet and want to do something to help you become more successful. Show signs of poverty and the entire world will try to take away that which you have of value. You can borrow money at the bank when you are prosperous and do not need it, but try and arrange a loan when you are poverty-stricken, or when some great emergency faces you! You are the master of your own destiny because you control the one thing which can change and redirect the course of human destinies, the power of thought. Let this great truth sink into your consciousness and this book will have marked the most important turning point of your life.

A MESSAGE TO THOSE WHO HAVE TRIED AND THOUGHT THEY FAILED!

The author would not be satisfied to send this book out on its mission of inspirational service without adding this short chapter as a personal message to those who have tried and 'failed'! Failure is such a mis-understood word. What chaos and distress and poverty and heartaches have come out of misinterpretation of this word!

Just a few days ago, the author stood on a humble spot of ground in the mountains of Kentucky, not far from his own birthplace, where a well-known 'failure' was born. When a very young man, this 'failure' went away to war, commissioned as a captain. His record was so poor that he was demoted to corporal and finally returned home as a private.

He took up surveying, but he could not make a living at this work and very soon he was humiliated by having his instruments sold for his debts. Next he took up law, but he got very few cases, and most of these he lost on account of incompetence. He became engaged to a young lady, but changed his mind and failed to show up for the wedding. He drifted into politics and by chance was elected to Congress, but his record was so drab that it caused no favourable comment. Everything he undertook brought him humiliation and failure.

Then a miracle happened! A great love experience came into his life, and despite the fact that the girl who aroused this love passed beyond the Great Divide, the lingering thoughts of that love caused this 'Nobody' to fight his way out of his humble role as failure, and, at the age of 52, he became the greatest and most beloved President who ever occupied the White House.

People are made, or broken, according to the use they make of the power of thought. Failure may be transformed into success overnight when one becomes inspired with a great impelling motive to succeed. The eight basic motives that move people to action have been described in a previous chapter. One of these eight is the motive of love. Abraham Lincoln's love for Anne Rutledge turned mediocrity into greatness. He found himself through the sorrow that came to him through her death.

Henry Ford was at one time the richest and most powerful man alive. He had to master poverty, illiteracy and other handicaps that the average man never encounters. He became successful because of the love inspired by a truly great woman, his wife, and this despite the fact that his early biographers never mentioned her name.

Every Ford car, the Ford millions, every Ford factory and all that Henry Ford accomplished for the good of humankind may be appropriately submitted as evidence of the soundness of the Law of Success philosophy, as he was the most practical student of this philosophy. From his life work, more than from any other source, has come the material that made this philosophy a reality.

The seed of all success lies sleeping in well-defined motive! Without a burning desire to achieve, superinduced by one or more of the eight basic motives, no one ever becomes a genius. Motivated by a highly developed sex life, Napoleon became the greatest leader of men of his time. His ignoble ending was the result of his lack of observance of two of the other 17 factors of success, namely self-control and the Golden Rule.

Lester Park entered the movie business at about the same time that the author began the organisation of the Law of Success philosophy. The 'miracle' that transformed Mr Park from a self-styled 'failure' into an outstanding success was described in an editorial written by the author and published in a New York newspaper. This editorial is here reproduced in full as a fitting close for this chapter.

Another Miracle

For 25 years I have been studying, measuring and analysing human beings. My research has brought me in contact with over 20,000 men and women. Two people out of this vast army stand out in bold contrast with nearly all the others. These two are Henry Ford and Lester Park.

Mr Ford's general average (measuring his commitment to the Laws of Success) was 95 per cent. Lester Park's general average was 94 per cent. When I first analysed Henry Ford, his rating on the 17 factors of success was 67 per cent. His gradual rise from 67 per cent to 95 per cent was an outstanding achievement, but nothing to compare with the transformation that took place in Lester Park's mental machinery over a period of but a few weeks.

When I first analysed Mr Park, his general average was 45 per cent. Less than a month later I made a second analysis and lo! He had jumped from 'zero' to 100 per cent on two of the most important of the 17 factors of success, and had made astounding advances in many of the other factors.

A Sweeping Endorsement

This analysis chart, showing Lester Park's two ratings on the factors that create power and wealth, is a sweeping endorsement of the belief that many philosophers have held: that all success is merely a state of mind! That people are lifted to great heights of power, or dashed into oblivion, solely by the thoughts they release on the wings of the ether.

Solitary Confinement

Lester Park was formerly one of the most active movie executives in America. His name was linked with those of others who have since made huge fortunes out of this business. But something 'snapped' in Lester Park's mental machinery. He lost his grip on himself. His self-confidence dropped to zero. He ceased to have a Definite Chief Aim. He drew himself away from contact with others in his profession, thereby depriving himself of the greatest of all the Laws of Success, the Master Mind (a mind that is a composite of two or more minds working in perfect harmony, for the attainment of some definite objective).

For years Lester Park committed himself, figuratively and literally, to solitary confinement in a dark dungeon! That dungeon was his own mind and he, himself, needed to find the key to the door.

The Wheel of Fate

Some time ago I conducted a class on the Laws of Success at the Waldorf-Astoria Hotel in New York City. By a strange turn of the wheel of chance – or was it the 'wheel of fate'? – Lester Park became a student in that class. The transformation that has taken place in Lester Park occurred in a fractional part of a minute, during the first half hour of my first lecture! In a single sentence I made a statement that served as a key that unlocked the door to the cell in which Lester Park had confined himself, and he stepped out, ready to pick up the reins where he had laid them down several years ago. The transformation is no imaginary one. It has been both real and complete.

Within two weeks, Lester Park had completed all arrangements for the production of one of the greatest pictures of his career. When I say he had 'completed all arrangements', I mean just that!

The money for the production was offered to him
from more than one source. Friends whom he had
known in the heyday of his career as a producer
suddenly appeared upon the scene as if by magic,
and greeted him like long-lost brothers! The
dream movie of his life became a living, pulsating
reality, and that picture is now in preparation for
production.

A Modern Miracle Had Happened!

That miracle brings great joy to my heart because
it proves, once more, that the child of my heart
and brain – the Law of Success philosophy – is
destined to emancipate millions of other Lester
Parks from the dark dungeons of despair to which
they have confined themselves. Many years ago,
Andrew Carnegie gave me an idea that caused me
to start a long period of labour and research. That
idea was the hub around which the Law of
Success philosophy has been built. I have lived to
see it bring freedom to countless millions, and to
how many more it will bring similar freedom I
have no way of knowing because the philosophy
is now being studied in nearly every civilised
country on earth, by those of every background,
with whom I have not personally come in
contact.

The man who sows a single beautiful thought in the mind of another renders the world, through that act, a greater service than that rendered by all the fault-finders combined.

A Prophecy Fulfilled

Years ago, when I predicted that Henry Ford would one day become the most powerful man on earth, my statement caused me great embarrassment because Ford had not then shown any signs of becoming the world's richest man. I stood behind that prediction and lived to see it become more than justified.

EDITOR'S NOTE
TO THE FIRST
EDITION

The book you've just read is made under the personal signature of Napoleon Hill, author of the Law of Success philosophy. Those who do not know of Mr Hill or his work are entitled to know that he has been engaged, for almost a quarter of a century, in experimenting with the human mind. In his research he has had valuable assistance from the best-known scientists of the world, such men as the late Alexander Graham Bell, Chas. P. Steinmetz and Luther Burbank. In a series of articles appearing in *McClure's* magazine, Henry Ford publicly admitted that the philosophy outlined in Mr Hill's 17 Laws of Success had been the foundation of his own rise to power and wealth.

Mr Hill is the Success Editor of the *New York Evening*

Graphic, and his 'Success Column' is appearing in other newspapers. Through this column he has kindled anew the fires of enthusiasm and ambition in the minds of thousands of men and women who had all but lost hope of achieving financial success.

The late Elbert H. Gary, former Chairman of the Board of the United States Steel Corporation, was preparing, at the time of his death, to present the Law of Success course to every employee of the steel corporation who could read English, at a total cost of something like $150,000.

Cyrus H.K. Curtis, owner of *The Saturday Evening Post* and one of the most successful publishers of the world, openly endorsed Mr Hill's discoveries and asked permission to reprint material from one of the lessons in the *Philadelphia Public Ledger.*

William Howard Taft, former President of the United States, endorsed the Law of Success philosophy in a most enthusiastic letter that Mr Hill received from him.

Edwin C. Barnes, a business associate of Thomas A. Edison, not only endorsed the Law of Success philosophy, and gave it credit for enabling him to retire from business with all the wealth he wanted at the age of 45, but also gave a most sweeping endorsement of Mr Hill personally, whom he has known for 20 years.

From this it may be said, without exaggeration, that Napoleon Hill is one of the great thinkers of the age – because no man could possibly command the respect and secure the endorsement of such men as those who have endorsed him, unless he were a sound thinker.

This is an Age of Action!

Summarising the 17 factors of success described in this volume, the reader may better grasp the entire philosophy by keeping in mind the fact that success is based upon power; that power is knowledge expressed in action.

All of the major stimuli which arouse the mind and put it into action have been described in this volume. The main purpose of the 17 factors of success is that of providing one with practical plans and methods of application for the use of these stimuli.

Careful analysis has disclosed the startling fact that a single incident, or experience, often results in such marked influence upon a mind of the most mediocre type that the owner of that mind surpasses, in achievement, others who have superior and better-trained minds.

The Law of Success, as described through the 17 factors outlined in this volume, provides all the known methods of mind stimulation that inspire the individual with high ambition and supply the courage essential for the attainment of the object of that ambition.

It is hardly sufficient to say that one may achieve more if one will undertake more. The author has aimed to offer the individual a practical mind stimulant, or source of inspiration, which may be used to build greater ambition and supply the motive for action in carrying out that ambition.

Ninety-five per cent of the energy of the human mind remains passive throughout life. The major purpose of this philosophy of success is to supply the stimuli that will arouse this sleeping 95 per cent of mind energy and put it to work. How? By planting in the mind some strong motive that will lead to action. By stepping up the mind, through contact with other minds, and causing it to vibrate on a higher plane.

INDEX

Also available from Vermilion by Napoleon Hill:

Think and Grow Rich

The essential guide to joining the ranks of the world's most successful people

Think and Grow Rich is the seminal work by the well-loved and world-renowned Napoleon Hill, a contemporary of Dale Carnegie. Originally published in 1937 and revised and updated for the 21st century, Hill's money-making secrets are as powerful today as they were then. After interviewing over 500 of the most affluent men and women of his time, Napoleon Hill uncovered the secret to great wealth based on the notion that if we can learn to think like the rich we can discover wealth and success. He developed a simple but powerful 13-step formula to help you to:

- identify your goals
- master the secret of true and lasting success
- obtain whatever you want in life
- join the ranks of the super-successful

This edition also provides examples of men and women who, in recent times, exemplify the principles that Hill put forward, including the success stories of top achievers such as Bill Gates and Steven Spielberg. Do you want to achieve your dreams? Then just follow Napoleon Hill's immortal rules.

'The first step to devising a winning strategy' *Sunday Times*

978 0 09 1900212
£8.99

Master Key to Riches:
The Secret to Making your Fortune

Unlock the door to your fortune using the secrets revealed in this book

Based on Andrew Carnegie's famous formula for money-making, *Master Key to Riches* has been revised and updated for the 21st century. As well as explaining the practical philosophy for success, in this inspiring book Napoleon Hill describes the key that will convert all your past failures into priceless assets and lead you to the attainment of the twelve great riches.

Drawing on the experiences of hundreds of the world's most powerful and wealthy people, this book will show you how to succeed in any walk of life.

978 0 09 191707 4
£8.99